Ethics for Behavior Analysts

*A Practical Guide
to the Behavior Analyst Certification
Board Guidelines for Responsible Conduct*

Ethics for Behavior Analysts

*A Practical Guide
to the Behavior Analyst Certification
Board Guidelines for Responsible Conduct*

Jon S. Bailey
Florida State University

Mary R. Burch
Board Certified Behavior Analyst

Routledge
Taylor & Francis Group
New York   London

Routledge
Taylor & Francis Group
270 Madison Avenue
New York, NY 10016

Routledge
Taylor & Francis Group
2 Park Square
Milton Park, Abingdon
Oxon OX14 4RN

DEDICATED TO: *John Jacobson (1949-2004) who showed us through his honesty, compassion, dedication and leadership what it means to be an ethical behavior analyst.*

© 2005 by Taylor & Francis Group, LLC
Routledge is an imprint of Taylor & Francis Group, an Informa business

Printed in the United States of America on acid-free paper
15 14 13 12 11 10 9 8 7 6
International Standard Book Number-13: 978-0-8058-5118-2 (Softcover)

Cover design by Kathryn Houghtaling Lacey. Cover photo by Jon S. Bailey, featuring Mary Kate Lettera, Alex Vergara and Marilyn McGhee. Printed with permission.

Library of Congress Cataloging-in-Publication Data
Bailey, Jon S. Ethics for behavior analysts : a practical guide to the Behavior Analyst Certification
  Board : guidelines for responsible conduct / Jon S. Bailey, Mary R. Burch.
      p. cm.
  Includes bibliographical references and index.
  ISBN 0-8058-5117-8 (cloth : alk. paper) ISSBN 0-8058-5118-6 (pbk. : alk. paper)
    1. Behavioral assessment—Moral and ethical aspects—United States—Handbooks, manual, etc.
    2. Behavior analysts—Professional ethics—United States—Handbooks, manuals, etc.
  RC473.B43B355 2005
  174.2'0973—dc22   2004061977

Visit the Taylor & Francis Web site at
http://www.taylorandfrancis.com

and the Routledge Web site at
http://www.routledge.com

Contents

PART III   Tips and Exercises for Students

Preface

EVOLUTION OF THIS BOOK AND HOW TO USE IT

My first experience in ethics came when I was a graduate student in psychology in the late 1960s. I was working with a profoundly developmentally disabled young man who was confined to a heavy metal crib in the small ward of a private institution in Phoenix, Arizona. Blind, deaf, nonambulatory, and not toilet trained, my "subject" engaged in self-injurious behavior virtually all day long. His head-banging behavior against the metal bars could be heard twenty-five yards away and greeted me each time I entered his depressing, malodorous living unit. Day after day, I sat by his crib taking notes on a possible thesis concerning how one might try to reduce his chronic self-injurious behavior or SIB (we called it *self-destructive behavior* in those days). After a few informal observation sessions, and reading through his medical chart, I had some ideas. I set up a meeting with one of my committee members, Dr. Lee Meyerson, who was supervising the research at the facility. "I'm observing a subject who engages in self-destructive behavior," I began. "He hits his head 10 to 15 times per minute throughout the day. I've taken informal data at different times of the day and I don't see any consistent pattern," I offered. Dr. Meyerson let me go on for about 10 minutes, nodding and occasionally taking a puff on his pipe (smoking was allowed everywhere in those days). Then he stopped me abruptly and gesturing with his pipe began to ask me questions that I had never thought about. Did I know my "subject's" name? Did I have permission to observe and report on this individual? Who gave me permission to look at this medical record? Had I discussed this case with any of my graduate student colleagues or shown the data in class? I had no good answers to any of Dr. Meyerson's questions. I wasn't thinking of my "subject" as a person, only as a source of data for my thesis. It never dawned on me that "Billy" had rights to privacy and confidentiality and that he needed to be treated with dignity and respect not as just another "subject" to help me complete a masters thesis. As it turns out, Dr. Meyerson was ahead of his time in grilling me with ethical questions that would not actually come up in legal circles for another ten years (see chap. 1). Dr. Meyerson's questions helped sensitize me to looking at what I was doing from an extra-experimental perspective. How would I like to be treated if I was a "subject" in someone's experiment? Or, how would I want my mother or sister to be treated? "With kindness, compassion and respect," is no doubt the quick response that most of us would offer. And so it is that ethics in psychology, and particularly in behavior analysis, can be easily personalized and made tangible if we will just stop and think about what we are doing.

Students today have a great advantage over my generation. We had no code of ethics or guidelines to follow; we had one foot in the animal lab and one in the real world and we were trying to figure out how to transform powerful operant conditioning principles into effective treatments. It didn't dawn on us at the time that ethics was involved at all, until of course, we encountered Dr. Lee Meyerson. Today, graduate students in behavior analysis have nearly thirty years of applied research and practice to fall back on (and to learn from and be held accountable for knowing). In addition, they have a wealth of resources on ethics including case law and precedent-setting legal findings. Finally, students today have a perfectly legitimate, thoroughly researched, and well-vetted set of guidelines specifically designed for our field: The Behavior Analyst Certification Board® (BACB) Guidelines for Responsible Conduct. In teaching the graduate course "Professional and Ethical Issues in

Behavior Analysis" for the past five years, I have learned a great deal about the ethical issues that appear to be unique to our field (see chap. 3) and have been developing lectures and trying to discover ways of making ethics interesting, informative, and engaging for students who do not quite see the relevance or appreciate our cautious approach. One thing I've discovered is that although we now have an excellent set of Guidelines, they are somewhat dry and by themselves do not convey the urgency and relevance that they should. Reading the Guidelines is something like reading instructions for computer software: it's clearly important but you would rather just start using it.

A few years ago, I was scheduled to give a half-day workshop at Penn State on ethics with Dr. Jerry Shook. In the process of preparing my materials, I wondered what kind of ethical questions the participants might have. Dr. Shook arranged in advance to have each participant write and submit to us two questions or "scenarios" that he or she had confronted in the work setting. When I got the questions, I realized that reading the scenarios suddenly made the ethical issues jump right off the page. I began trying to look up the correct responses (according to the BACB® Guidelines), and this turned out to be quite difficult. Something was missing, an index of some sort would help, but none was available that I could find. Several all-nighters later, I had developed one. By the time Dr. Shook and I traveled to the conference, I had a new approach to teaching ethics. It involved presenting scenarios, having the students look up the relevant sections in the Guidelines, and then present their proposed ethical actions. This approach teaches students that sometimes broad, ethical considerations always come down to some specific Guidelines. My experience in using this method over the past several years is that it brings the topic to life and generates excellent discussions of very relevant issues.

One troubling problem I encountered in teaching the "Ethics for Behavior Analysis" course was that specific code items were often very much out of context, or written in such stilted legalese that students did not understand why they were necessary or how they were relevant. I found myself often "translating" specific Guidelines into plain English. This process, along with providing some historic context and background about how and why certain items were important in our field, seemed to increase the level of understanding for the students.

This book, then, is the culmination of this attempt to present a practical, student-centered approach to teaching ethics in behavior analysis. All of the cases are based on real examples known to the authors but modified so as to avoid embarrassment or legal hassles. In addition, for each case, there is a question for the student to consider followed by a response that can be found at the end of each chapter. In chapter 14, you will find eleven practice scenarios that can be used in class or as homework. You can of course, develop your own scenarios based on the specific areas of application that you encounter in your practice of behavior analysis. Our examples lean heavily on our experience in autism, developmental disabilities, education, and Organizational Behavior Management (OBM).

A final word about using this volume: this text is intended to be a practical handbook and we specifically attempted to avoid making this an academic or theoretical work. Although we feel that it is quite comprehensive, it is not intended to be used alone but rather as a supplement to other texts or sources that you are currently using (see Suggested Reading in Part III). Many people teaching ethics courses will routinely have students read the U.S. Constitution, view "One Flew Over the Cuckoo's Nest," and research their state laws on limits of treatment, requirements for keeping documents, maintaining confidentiality, and other relevant issues. My experience is that it takes some creative digging to find relevant readings. Exposing students to a variety of sources from Skinner and Sidman to Association for Behavior Analysis (ABA) position statements is useful in preparing them to tackle the world of ethical issues they will confront. I have tried to summarize what I consider the most important and pressing issues for new Board Certified Behavior Analysts (BCBAs) in chapter 14: "A Dozen Practical Tips for Ethical Conduct on Your First Job." I hope you enjoy using this book and welcome input and dialogue on effective ways of teaching this most important topic.

—*Jon S. Bailey*
October 10, 2004

ACKNOWLEDGMENTS

We would like to thank Cristal Elwood for her insightful comments and helpful editing suggestions on an earlier draft of this manuscript. We are also indebted to Jerry Shook. Without him and the Behavior Analyst Certification Board, there would be no Guidelines.

DISCLAIMER

This book does not represent an official statement by the Behavior Analyst Certification Board®, the Association for Behavior Analysis, or any other behavior analysis organization. This text cannot be relied on as the only interpretation of the meaning of the Guidelines or their application to particular situations. Each BCBA, supervisor, or relevant agency must interpret and apply the Guidelines as it believes proper, given all of the circumstances.

The cases used in this book are based on the authors' combined 50 years of experience in behavior analysis. Some are nearly exact representations of actual events whereas others are an amalgam of two or more incidents. In all cases, we have disguised the situations and used pseudonyms to protect the privacy of the parties and organizations involved. At the end of some of the chapters, we offer "Responses to Case Questions" as examples of real, or in some cases, hypothetical solutions to the ethical problems posed by the case. We do not hold these to be the only ethical solutions, but rather, each response is an example of one ethical solution. We encourage instructors who use the text to create alternate solutions based on their own experiences. Finally, we hope that the responses offered here will stimulate discussion, debate, and thoughtful consideration about ways of handling what are by definition very delicate matters.

I

Background for Ethics in Behavior Analysis

Chapter 1

How We Got Here

There is nothing more shocking and horrific than the abuse and mal-treatment of innocent people who are unable to protect and defend themselves. Atrocious incidents of physical and emotional abuse to-ward animals, children, women, and people who are elderly occur every single day in our culture and they are often reduced to a few lines in the local news of the daily paper.

Individuals who are developmentally disabled can also be the victims of abuse. The reprehensible mistreatment of children and adults with disabilities is especially disturbing when the abuses come at the hands of your chosen profession. But this is exactly what happened in Florida in the early 1970s. These abuses changed the course of history for behavior analysis and the treatment of people with disabilities.

The story of the evolution of guidelines for responsible conduct of be-havior analysts began in the late 1960s when "behavior modification" was all the rage. Having started only in the mid-1960s (Krasner & Ullmann, 1965; Neuringer & Michael, 1970; Ullmann & Krasner, 1965), some of behavior modification's early promoters promised dramatic changes in behavior that were quick and easy to produce and could be carried out by almost anyone with an attendance certificate from a day-long "behavior mod" workshop. People calling themselves "behavior modifiers" offered rented-hotel-ballroom training sessions in abun-dance. There were no prerequisites for registering and no questions were asked about the speaker's qualifications. The basic pitch was this: "You don't have to know why a behavior occurs (it was assumed to be learned—an 'operant behavior'), you only need to know how to manipulate consequences. Food is a primary reinforcer for almost everybody; just make it contingent on the behavior you want. For inappropriate or dangerous behavior use consequences (punishers) to 'decelerate' the behavior." There was no consideration given to the notion of "causes" of behavior or that there might be a connection between a likely cause and an effective treatment. Further, no thought was given to possible side effects of using food (e.g., food allergies, weight gain) or how the food, often candy, might be handled. Indeed, Cheerios®, M&Ms®, pretzels and other bite-sized snacks and treats were loaded in the pockets of the "behavior specialist" in the morning and used throughout the day as needed (a hungry behavior specialist might even have a few from time to time). Likewise, aversive consequences were used with abandon in informal, impromptu, and spontaneous reactions to self-injurious, destructive, and inappropriate behaviors. Some staff were urged to "be creative" in coming up with consequences. As a result, hot pepper sauces such as Tabasco®, and undiluted lemon juice, might be seen in the jacket pockets of staff members who were on their way to work on "the behavior unit."

In the early 1970s, "the unit" was frequently a residential facility for developmentally disabled individuals who had moderate to severe mental retardation, some physical disabilities, and troublesome behaviors. It was most likely a former veteran's or tuberculosis (TB) hospital, which might house 300 to 1,500 "patients." Custodial care was the norm until "behavior mod" came along and offered dramatic treatment for severe behavior problems. With no guidelines and essentially no restrictions, this "treatment" quickly drifted into flat-out abuse.

THE SUNLAND MIAMI SCANDAL

The Sunland Training Center in Miami became "ground zero" for an abuse investigation that rocked the state of Florida in 1972. The center had been plagued by high turnover rates since it opened in 1965, resulting in frequent understaffing and low-quality training. Surprisingly, the majority of students serving as "cottage parents" were college students. In 1969, the superintendent resigned under pressure from an investigation into "allegations of resident abuse." It seems that he confined two residents in a "cell improvised from a large trailer" (McAllister, 1972, p. 2). Then, in April 1971, the Florida Division of Mental Retardation and the Dade County Attorney's Office began an intensive investigation of resident abuse that concluded after a six-month inquiry regarding allegations of "infrequent and isolated cases of abuse" (p. 2) and that the superintendent had dealt with the employees involved and taken appropriate disciplinary action. One of those professional employees, Dr. E., challenged his reassignment and a grievance committee then uncovered what it considered to be a "highly explosive situation" involving resident abuse with the apparent knowledge and approval of top administrators. As a result, seven individuals were immediately suspended, including the superintendent, the director of Cottage Life, the staff psychologist, three cottage supervisors, and a cottage parent. Each was charged with "misfeasance, malfeasance, negligence, and contributing to the abuse of residents" (McAllister, 1972, p. 4). Subsequent to this, Jack McAllister, the director of the State Health and Rehabilitative Services (HRS) Division of Retardation, formed a nine-member Blue Ribbon Panel "Resident Abuse Investigating Committee" comprised of experts in retardation, as well as an attorney, a social worker, a client advocate, and two behavior analysts (Dr. Jack May, Jr., and Dr. Todd Risley). Interviews were set up with over 70 individuals, including current staff members, former employees, residents, and relatives of residents (including one whose son died at Sunland Miami), with some interviews lasting as long as ten hours. The committee also examined original logs, internal memoranda, a personal diary, and personnel records.

It seems that Dr. E., a psychologist who presented himself as an expert in behavior modification and joined the staff in 1971, had set up a truly ironically-named program called the "Achievement Division" in three cottages, allegedly to study "some rather esoteric questions of statistical models for economic analysis" (p. 15). Dr. E., over a period of the next year, established a "treatment" program that consisted of, or evolved

into, abusive incidents, including the following: forced public mastur-
bation (for residents caught masturbating), forced public homosexual
acts (again for those caught in the act), forced washing of the mouth
with soap (as punishment for lying, abusive language or simply speaking
at all), beatings with wooden paddle (10 "licks" for running away); excessive use of restraints, including one resident who was restrained for
more than twenty-four hours and another who was forced to sit in a
bathtub for two days. Restraints were routinely used as punishment
rather than an emergency method of preventing self-injury. As if this
were not enough, the list of horrific, systematic abuses goes on: a male
client required to wear women's underpants, excessive use of lengthy
(four-hour) seclusions in barren and unpadded rooms with no permission to leave to use the bathroom, public shaming by forcing a resident
to wear a sign that said "The Thief," food withheld as a form of punishment, sleep withheld as punishment, another resident forced to hold
feces-stained underwear under his nose for ten minutes as punishment
for incontinence, and another resident forced to lay on urine-soaked
sheets for repeated incontinence (McAllister, 1972, pp. 10–11).

The "milieu" of the Achievement Division consisted of an utter lack
of programmed activities, which resulted in "profound boredom and
deterioration, unattractive surroundings, complete lack of privacy,
public humiliation, nakedness ..., and lack of any means of residents to
express their grievances" (p. 13). One resident died from dehydration
and another drowned in a nearby canal in his futile attempt to escape his
cottage at Sunland Miami.

At first glance it might appear that such abuses would certainly have
to be the work of a few frustrated, angry, poorly trained employees bent
on sadistic acts. However, the investigation revealed to the contrary,
that these revolting acts of abuse were the result of an attempt by Dr. E.
to create a "superb behavior modification program" (p. 14) using routine "behavior shaping devices" (p. 15). The committee's explanation
was that this program "degenerated ... into a bizarre, abusive, and ineffective system of punishment" (p. 17). In the Achievement Division,
these procedures were systematically applied, condoned by supervisors
and professional staff and recorded in daily living unit logs. Not only

were the procedures used openly but they were, at least initially, well re-searched. A token program, for example, had been modeled after one first developed in Parsons, Kansas, by Dr. James Lent, a well-respected expert in behavioral treatment. One key ingredient was left out of this and other aspects of the Achievement Division: monitoring of individual resident behavior. Rather, the emphasis was on guidelines for treatment that gave the otherwise poorly-trained employees a great deal of latitude in their reactions. The three guidelines were as follows (McAllister, 1972): (a) emphasize "natural consequences of behavior," (b) devise your own immediate response to problem behaviors that might crop up where no other instructions apply, and (c) do not threaten—if you verbalize a consequence to a resident, "follow through on every contingency."

The investigating committee was adamant in its observation that none of the cruel and abusive procedures employed in the Achievement Division had any basis in the behavior modification literature or "any other modern therapeutic or educational methodology." They went on to suggest that because the cottage where the abuses took place was totally isolated from outside monitoring it was entirely possible for "well meaning but poorly trained personnel" to try some mild form of these procedures and then gradually escalate to the bizarre applications that were ultimately achieved. Each instance was, as noted previously, in a daily log book, and given no corrective action or response, a cottage parent would naturally assume tacit approval and then perhaps employ a "slightly more extreme form" of the procedure. "In this way, quite extreme procedures evolved in gradual steps from spontaneous initiation of less extreme procedures by the cottage staff, until ... a pattern had been established of dealing with recurrent problems by escalating the intensity of whatever procedures happened to be in use for a particular resident" (pp. 17–18). This natural tendency toward "behavior drift" on the part of the staff is certainly not uncommon in residential treatment facilities. In the case of Sunland Miami, it is was facilitated by a nearly total lack of monitoring by upper-level management. The written policies at Sunland Miami clearly prohibited abusive practices but there was no evidence that these were "forcefully communicated" to employees, and recall that the facility suffered from chronic turnover of staff so that ongoing staff training was superficial at best.

Another concern of the investigating committee had to do with the training and credentials of Dr. E. As it turns out, he had recently graduated with his doctoral degree from the University of Florida and then completed some postdoctorate work at Johns Hopkins University. He claimed to have worked with some of the biggest names in the field, but when the committee contacted them, these eminent researchers "vaguely remembered a brash young man who visited their laboratories on several occasions," but none would claim him as their student (p. 19). It must be remembered that Dr. E. was trained in the late 1960s when the field was in it's infancy, and it appeared that the sky was the limit as far as behavior modification was concerned. The *Journal of Applied Behavior Analysis,* the professional journal of behavior analysis, had only first been published in 1968, so there was very little research on the application of behavior principles and there was no code of ethics for behavioral researchers or practitioners.

RECOMMENDATIONS OF THE BLUE RIBBON COMMITTEE

The investigating committee took on itself the additional responsibility of making recommendations to hopefully prevent any future systematic abuses in the name of behavior modification in the state of Florida. These included strong support for a statewide advocacy program in which staff members would be allowed to make unannounced visits to residential institutions and collect information from key personnel as well as residents, parents, staff, and concerned citizens. In addition, the committee recommended professional peer review of all behavior programs to assure that treatment was derived from the literature and that no procedures would be used that were considered "experimental." Experimental programs would come under standard review for human experimentation in the HRS Division of Retardation. Other recommendations of the committee included the following: (a) the prohibition of certain bizarre examples of punishment, and (b) abandoning seclusion in favor of "positive and appropriate 'time out' techniques" (McAllister, 1972, p. 31).

FOLLOW-UP

In most cases, a report such as that produced by the Blue Ribbon Committee would simply find its way to the shelves of state bureaucrats and languish with no lasting effect. Such was not the case in Florida. The Florida Association for Retarded Children (now the Association for Retarded Citizens of Florida) took up the cause of humane treatment and ultimately endorsed the notion of supporting data-based, behavioral treatment, using strict guidelines, under close supervision by properly trained professionals. The Division of Retardation, under the guidance of Charles Cox, instituted reforms including setting up both statewide and local peer review committees for behavior modification programming in facilities throughout Florida. The Statewide Peer Review Committee for Behavior Modification (PRC) then established a set of guidelines for the use of behavioral procedures, which were subsequently adopted by the National Association for Retarded Citizens (MR Research, 1976) and by the Florida Division of Retardation as Health and Rehabilitative Services Manual (HRSM) 160–4 (May et al., 1976). The state-funded PRC proceeded to make visits to institutions around the state over the next several years educating staff members about the guidelines and making recommendations for more ethical treatment. By 1980, the PRC reached a consensus that it was time to encourage all the institutions, group homes, and smaller residential facilities to begin networking with one another and to begin to bring some sense of professionalism to behavior analysis in Florida. The "First Florida Work Session on Behavior Analysis in Retardation" was held in September of 1980 and drew nearly 300 administrators, treatment specialists, behavior analysts, and direct care staff to the two-day conference held in Orlando. At this historic conference, a meeting was held to organize an official state association. The first annual conference of the Florida Association for Behavior Analysis (FABA) was held in 1981, again in Orlando. None other than B. F. Skinner was the keynote speaker. The formation of the FABA marked a turning point in behavior analysis not only in Florida, but in the rest of the country. It was now possible to set high expectations for behavioral treatment because leaders in the field were routinely being brought to state conference to present their latest applied behavioral research, and practitioners had an opportunity to see firsthand what others were doing in other parts of the country to solve some of the most intractable behavior problems of the day. Administrators from state government and from private facilities were able to see that behavior analysis was not just some local phenomenon but rather an approach to treatment that was legitimate, effective, and humane. The PRC, in conjunction with the FABA, began the process of certifying behavior analysts via a testing program that was sponsored by the Division of Retardation. In 1988, the FABA membership adopted the FABA Code of Ethics, the first state association to do so.

THE SUNLAND MIAMI LEGACY

In retrospect, the horrific abuses at Sunland Miami in the early 1970s were probably necessary for half-baked, unregulated behavior modification to evolve into professional, respected, behavior analysis. Without the abuses, there would have been no Blue Ribbon Committee formed to think seriously about how to protect developmentally disabled individuals from systematic abuse of behavioral procedures. The headlines resulted in the intense scrutiny of a treatment mode that was in its infancy and that needed guidelines and oversight. The pain and suffering of the developmentally disabled individuals involved in the abuses amplified the need to think clearly about the ethics of treatment. Although it would have been easier to prohibit behavior modification altogether, the Blue Ribbon Committee was convinced by its two behavioral advocates, Drs. May and Risley, that a better alternative was to establish strict guidelines for treatment and to set up an infrastructure for oversight which involved community citizens who would bring their values, common sense, and good judgment to evaluate behavioral treatment strategies on an ongoing basis. The notion of oversight by both human rights and peer review committees gave teeth to the public appraisal of behavior analysis. These actions, plus the development of a state-endorsed mechanism of certification, the evolution of a strong state professional organization and its promotion of a Code of Ethics for Behavior Analysts, put in place all the necessary elements of control and management to prevent future abuses. And ethics, after all, is concerned primarily with the edict to "do no harm." In the Florida case, we saw how great harm could be done by well-meaning people, and that when appropriate, comprehensive strategies were adopted, abuse was prevented. Although ethics is usually seen as an individual professional engaging in responsible behavior of his or her own volition, the Florida case suggests that responsible conduct can be encouraged by other means as well. It is certainly painful and embarrassing for a profession to undergo such public scrutiny and scorn, but it was clearly warranted in this case. Indeed, it is hard to imagine such powerful procedures as behavioral treatments being used consistently across the board in the absence of such obvious forms of oversight and control.

It is also clear that even given these mechanisms, the behavior analyst faces numerous questions every day about the appropriateness of treatment decisions. What is fair? What is right? Am I qualified to administer this treatment? Can I do no harm? Am I taking enough data? Am I interpreting it correctly? Would my client be better off with no treatment? It is the purpose of this volume to try and elucidate the current Behavior Analyst Certification Board (BACB) Guidelines for Responsible Conduct to assist the behavior analyst in making right choices on a daily basis.

Chapter 2

Core Ethical Principles

Behavior analysts are part of a culture of caring individuals who seek to improve the lives of others. They carry with them a set of core ethical values that are derived from thousands of years of compassionate practices dating back to the Greeks. (Ethics comes from the Greek word *ethos,* meaning moral character.) As a field, ethics can be divided into three divisions: normative ethics, meta-ethics, and practical ethics. Although it is the purpose of this volume to focus on practical ethics in behavior analysis, we first need to discuss some basic moral principles that underlie our culture at large. These core ethical principles guide our everyday lives and play a significant role in basic decision making in the practice of our profession.

In 1998, Koocher and Keith-Spiegel outlined nine ethical principles for psychologists. These principles can be applied to ethics in many areas, including psychology, the teaching of children, and the training of animals. Koocher and Keith-Spiegel's nine core ethical principles are so basic, yet often go unstated, that we listed them, following, with explanations of how they relate to behavior analysis:

1. Do No Harm—The expression, "First, do no harm," is usually attributed to Hippocrates, a Greek physician in the fourth century B.C. Commonly written as "Do no harm," the phrase is typically re-

ferred to as appearing in the Hippocratic Oath that is taken by physicians. However, there is some debate on this issue (Harvard Classics, vol. 38, 1910). Hippocrates did say, "As to diseases, make a habit of two things—to help, or at least to do no harm." The Hippocratic Oath states, "I will follow that system of regimen which, according to my ability and judgment, I consider for the benefit of my patients, and abstain from whatever is deleterious and mischievous."

Although no behavior analyst would knowingly do harm, it can come in subtle forms that need to be attended to carefully. One obvious example is that of a behavior analyst who is practicing outside his or her area of expertise.

CASE EXAMPLE 1

A behavior analyst who has been trained to work with adolescents accepts the case of a preschool child who is having severe tantrums at school. His initial impression is that the child is "noncompliant" and he prepares a behavior program based on extinction of tantrum behaviors plus a DRO for compliance.

Another form of "harm" might come in a more subtle case of the behavior analyst who does not develop a responsible data collection system and misses the significance of a behavior.

CASE EXAMPLE 2

A certified behavior analyst (CBA) consulting with a group home receives a referral for a young developmentally-disabled man who is described as engaging in "self-stimulatory behavior." He asks the staff to begin data collection which involves counting the num-

*ber of incidents per day. Two weeks later he reviews the baseline
data and tells staff members that they do not have a significant
problem and not to worry because the behavior is only occurring
two to three times per day. On his next visit, the CBA inquires
about the client only to discover that he was taken to the emergency room with lacerations to his scalp requiring six stitches. A
review of the case determined that the CBA failed to inquire about
the severity of the behaviors and failed to ask the nursing staff to
perform skin ratings.*

Behavior analysts are often working with staff members who are not
at all well versed in human behavior and who will not necessarily think
to offer all the information necessary to operate ethically.

CASE EXAMPLE 3: HERMAN

*Herman was referred for his combative behavior when being
guided toward the shower each morning in a residential facility
for the developmentally disabled. He was reluctant to take a
shower and showed his displeasure by pushing and shoving the
staff and trying to escape. This resulted in at least two staff injuries, one in the shower itself that left the training instructor unable
to work for two weeks. Clearly this was a case of aggressive behavior that needed treatment. In light of the danger involved, the staff
strongly recommended restraint as an immediate consequence for
Herman's refusal to cooperate with his morning bathing routine.
This program was nearly implemented when the behavior analyst
inquired about how long this problem had been going on. The answer turned the treatment in a totally different direction. It turned
out that Herman had previously been allowed to take his bath at
night, and was assisted by an aide who helped him by filling up the
tub, getting just the right temperature for the water, providing his
favorite towel, and in general, recreating the conditions his*

mother used at home. When this staff member quit the facility, it was determined that Herman should take a shower in the morning, which, as we came to understand, he detested. Although it was possible that a behavior program could have been written to essentially force Herman to take a morning shower, it was determined that this would cause more harm than good. The ethical solution for this case was to train another staff member to re-instate Herman's evening bath.

2. Respecting autonomy—To respect one's autonomy means to promote his or her independence or self-sufficiency. Clearly the basic procedures of behavior analysis are designed to do just this: prompting, shaping, chaining, fading and the use of conditioned reinforcers, token economies and prosthetic environments are all designed to change behavior in such a way that the person can deliver his or her own reinforcers rather than depend on a mediator. Clashes can occur, of course, when it is determined that someone actually prefers to keep another under their control. This can produce very difficult situations for the behavior analyst who is often hired by that person.

CASE EXAMPLE 4: MOLLY

Molly was a cute, dimple-cheeked four-year-old with language delay. She was receiving one-on-one therapy each day from a certified associate behavior analyst. The therapist was making progress in teaching Molly basic sounds for common objects. She was confronted by the mother who was clearly not happy with the treatment. It seems that Molly now knew the names for milk, cookie, snack, draw, play with blocks, and a few other words and she was beginning to generalize these requests to the mother. The mother's position was that Molly would get snacks only when she wanted her to have them. By learning to request these items, the

*mother was afraid that Molly would become pushy and demand-
ing. "The next thing you know she will think that she can just get
in the fridge and get her own drinks," said Molly's mother.*

Autonomy can also bring risks that cannot always be foreseen. A behavior analyst who advocates for a person to acquire a skill that will provide greater independence has to recognize that this may put the person
in harm's way.

CASE EXAMPLE 5: MARIE

*Marie was a geriatric patient in a nursing home. She spent most of
her day in bed refusing to participate in most activities. The goal of
the facility was to encourage patients to ambulate independently
when possible and to attend the wide variety of social and cultural
events that were offered. The behavior analyst reviewed Marie's
case and determined that she was capable of walking with assistance but got more reinforcement from refusing. After determining Marie's reinforcers, the behavior analyst arranged to make
them contingent on first walking with assistance and then, after
approval of the physical therapist, walking on her own. The case
was considered a success until Marie fell and broke a hip. Marie's
family considered the behavior analyst responsible for this acci-
dent. One family member said, "Why didn't you just leave well
enough alone? She preferred to stay in bed but you had to meddle
in her affairs."*

Behavior analysts often work in educational or business settings
where they consult in the areas of classroom management or performance management. In these settings, the notion of autonomy can also
produce some ethical issues. For example, teachers are frequently reinforced by the students who stay in their seats and follow instructions;

business managers and supervisors may desire that their employees simply "follow directions" and do what they are told.

CASE EXAMPLE 6: RORY

Rory supervised 15 employees in a small machine shop that fabricated specialized exhaust systems for racing cars. His employees were well paid and creative in coming up with solutions for the increasingly complex demands of their elite customers. After attending a conference on Performance Management (PM), Rory contacted one of the speakers and asked for help. What he wanted was for his employees to follow the manual that he had written a few years earlier. "These young guys think they know it all. They are coming up with completely new designs and telling our customers that my methods are outdated."

---

3. Benefiting Others—It almost goes without saying that the primary role of behavior analysts is to benefit others in whatever setting or situation they may work. This principle can often put the behavior analyst at odds with other professionals and requires frequent checks on "who is the client?" in any given situation.

CASE EXAMPLE 7: TAMARA AND MS. HARRIS

Tamara was referred to the behavior analyst by her teacher. Tamara's problem was that she caused frequent disturbances in the classroom. Her teacher, Ms. Harris, provided a data sheet showing date, time, and type of disturbance going back two weeks. Ms. Harris requested help in setting up a time-out booth for Tamara. Although Ms. Harris was the person requesting help, the behavior analyst quickly determined that Tamara was her client and she decided to take her own data. This required several visits to the school, which was quite a distance from the rest of the behavior analyst's cases. Tamara benefited from this extra effort on the part of the behavior analyst because it was discovered that her classroom disturbances were due to a hearing problem and not "willfulness," as alleged by the teacher.

4. Being Just—This principle is very basic and is directly derived from the "Golden Rule" or the Ethic of Reciprocity (Ontario Consultants on Religious Tolerance, 2004). Being just means that you should treat others as you would like to be treated. This has special meaning in behavior analysis because there is some potential for the use of uncomfortable stimuli or stressful contingencies in treatment. A further refinement of the ethic might ask, "How would I like my mother or my child to be treated in similar circumstances?" Questions of just treatment arise often in behavior analysis because there is often so little known about the origins of a particular behavior and functional relationships often assumed are yet to be determined.

CASE EXAMPLE 8

A senior behavior analyst was asked to consult on the case of a client who was engaging in persistent self-injurious behavior—arm and face scratching. Ignoring had been tried without effect and a fairly dense DRO with blocking was not proving effective either. The behavior analyst was puzzled but asked himself, "How would I like to be treated?" and realized that he had been treated for just such a behavior about two years prior. He had been diagnosed with a case of hives (his scratching looked a lot like Self Injurious Behavior) and felt fortunate to receive medication rather than a "DRO plus blocking." The behavior analysts' attention then turned to medical diagnosis of the client's "SIB."

5. Being Truthful Well-respected professionals attain their reputation based on the trust placed in them by others. Those who are loyal, trustworthy, and honest are sought out as dependable and reliable sources of wise counsel and effective, ethical treatment. Being truthful and honest with clients, colleagues, and administrators provides the basis for long-term relationships that make for a successful career.

CASE EXAMPLE 9: DR. B

Dr. B., an experienced behavior analyst, was consulting at a residential facility for clients with behavior problems that were severe enough to prevent them from living at home or in the community. One day, as soon as Dr. B. arrived at the facility, the administrator approached him and began congratulating him on successfully treating one of the most intransient cases in the facility. After discussions with the behavior specialist and Certified Associate Behavior Analyst (CABA), Dr. B. met with the administrator to explain that no credit was due. In fact, baseline was still underway and the treatment plan had not yet been executed.

---

6. According Dignity—Many of the clients that we serve are not able to effectively represent themselves. They may be nonverbal or simply unable to get someone to listen to them. If their wishes are unknown and they are unable to make choices, they may become depressed and present behavior problems which come to the attention of a behavior analyst. Although it is not a "behavioral" term, low self-esteem seems to capture the essence of a person who has not been afforded dignity. As behavior analysts, our job is to make sure that each and every client IS treated with dignity and respect. Behaviorally this means that we would work with clients on acquisition skills to make sure that they are able to voice or signal their needs to those around them. A good behavior analyst would also

push for all staff to undergo the training necessary to learn to communicate with the clients who are nonverbal. These persons should be given choices throughout the day and allowed to exercise their preferences for food, clothing, roommate, activities, and living conditions. Other more subtle ways of according dignity involve the language we use to talk to or about clients. If you want to know how Bertha feels about her treatment plan, you could ask the staff or family or you could ask Bertha herself. Clients should be addressed by name in a friendly fashion using eye contact and a pleasant smile—the kind of treatment you expect when you are receiving services from someone in your business community.

CASE EXAMPLE 10: THOMAS

Thomas was a nonverbal, developmentally-disabled young man who was referred for his aggressive and sometimes self-injurious behavior. The incidents seemed to occur in the afternoon when he returned to his group home from his sheltered work setting. It often took two staff members to drag him from his bedroom to the living room where there were group activities. Before being taken to the living room, he had to be dressed because he was frequently found sitting in his underwear on the floor rocking and listening to music on his headset. After some considerable investigation and discussion with staff, family, nurses, and social workers, the behavior analyst prevailed in his position that Thomas should be given his choice of activities in the afternoon. He was to be offered the option of joining the group each day but if he chose to stay in his room and listen to music, his choice was respected. Given this resolution there was no need to develop a behavior treatment program because the aggressive and self-injurious behavior ceased to exist.

---

7. Treating others with caring and compassion—Many of the previous ethical principles relate to this ethical principle. If, as a behavior

analyst, you respect the autonomy of clients, work to benefit them, and devise programs that accord them dignity, you will automatically be treating clients with care and compassion. This value also suggests not only that clients be given choices but that interpersonal relationships should demonstrate sympathy and concern.

CASE EXAMPLE 11: TERRENCE

Terrence hated getting up in the morning to go to work. He would fight with staff members, throw shoes at them, and pull the bed covers up over his head. One staff member who reported no such reaction when she was on duty described her method of getting Terrence up. "Basically I try to treat him like my dad who lives with us. He's on medication just like Terrence, and I know that it makes him groggy in the morning. So, I have to show some patience with Terrence. What I do is I go in his room and say in my sweetest voice, 'Terrence honey, it's almost time to get up,' and I open the curtains about half way and then I leave his room. Then I come back about 15-minutes later and open them the rest of the way and go to Terrence and gently rub his arm and say, 'How you doin' Terrence? It's almost time to get up. We've got some fresh coffee brewing and I've set out your favorite work clothes. I'll be back to get you in a few minutes.' Then about 15-minutes after that I come back and if he's not up I turn on his clock radio and say, 'Terrence sweetheart, it's time to get up now. Here let me help you get dressed.' I know this takes extra effort but this is the way I would like to be treated and it's the way I treat my dad so I don't mind. And it works. By the time I turn on the radio he's swinging out of bed and has that little half-grin on his face that says 'Thank you for being so understanding.' "

8. Pursuit of Excellence—Behavior analysis is a rapidly growing field. Behavior analysts need to stay current with new developments

as well as constantly updated rules and regulations. Excellence in this profession means being aware of the latest research in the field and in your specialty and incorporating the most up-to-date methods and procedures in your practice of behavior analysis. It is a given that you will subscribe to the key journals in the field and attend your state association meeting as well as the annual meeting of the Association for Behavior Analysis. To stay at the top of your game, you may also want to watch for specialty workshops offered in your area or consider taking graduate seminars offered at a nearby university. The BACB® requires CBA's to acquire continuing education each year. Continuing education hours required by the BACB are a minimum and the behavior analyst who wants to maintain excellence will set aside two to four hours each week to read the latest journals and newest reference works.

CASE EXAMPLE 12: NORA

Nora received her master's degree in psychology with a specialty in applied behavior analysis in the mid-1990s. Since then she has gone to a few conferences but does not find them exciting enough to maintain her interest. She was embarrassed recently at a local peer review meeting when a newly-minted PhD began questioning her proposed treatment plans. She had not been aware of new standards for functional assessment and was surprised to find that she was so out of touch.

---

9. Accepting Responsibility—Behavior analysts have an awesome responsibility in analyzing the behavior of a client and then making recommendations to implement a program to change a target behavior. In pursuing excellence, you will want to make sure that everything you have done in making your diagnosis is of the highest standard. By presenting your conclusions to colleagues and other professionals, you are responsible for making sure that the proposed

treatment is proper, justified, and worthy of consideration. And, when your treatments fail, you must take responsibility, accepting blame and making corrections to satisfy the consumer and other related parties. Behavior analysts who are better at making excuses than analyzing behavior do the profession no favor. Those who do not take the time to research the problem they are working on and arrive at hasty conclusions will find themselves constantly in the line of fire.

CASE EXAMPLE 13: CLARA

Clara had only been on her job for three-months when she found herself at the center of a serious discussion at an Individual Education Plan (I.E.P.) meeting at one of the schools where she worked. She developed a token economy for one of the teachers to use with a student. The program involved the teacher giving the student points for quietly doing her work. Unfortunately, Clara failed to take into account the issue of quality when writing up the child's program and now the teacher was very irritated at Clara claiming that "she has created a monster who cares nothing for the work and just scribbles away on her papers so that she can get her stupid points." Rather than point out the rather obvious fact that the teacher could have easily made the decision to reward only quality work, Clara accepted responsibility, apologized to the teacher, and rewrote the program.

Behavior analysts do not begin their ethical training in graduate school. A person's ethical training begins long before the college years. Developmental psychologists would argue that one's ethical standards are fairly well set by the time a child ventures into junior high school. Personal ethical situations confront people every day and there is probably a tendency to generalize from these everyday occurrences to professional life. A person who advances his or her own personal interests above others, avoids conflict, and does not take responsibility for his or her actions, is unlikely to immediately take account of ethical standards in his or her profession. It is for these reasons that a Code of Responsible Conduct has been developed for behavior analysts. It is our hope that by reviewing these principles and examining the Code carefully, behavior analysts will come to see the value in adopting a set of responsible behaviors that will advance the profession and provide respect to this important new field of psychology.

Chapter 3

What Makes Behavior Analysis Unique?

In many respects, the practice of behavior analysis is unique, as compared to those of the other helping professions. Although other fields may represent that they base their treatment methods on science, behavior analysis is the only human services approach to actually take the next step and require that the treatment itself use these methods. This is possible because the methodology is founded on single-subject design research where each individual serves as his or her own control (Bailey & Burch, 2002). In research studies, this means that baseline data is collected for each participant and interventions are applied and evaluated for each person individually. This strategy is maintained in the therapy that is derived from the science, that is, each client is evaluated individually, custom-tailored measurement is designed for each person based on the referred behavior, and online evaluation of the intervention is made continuously until the case is terminated. To complicate matters, the field of behavior analysis encompasses a very wide range of clients (some call them *consumers*) that have to be served ranging from very low functioning, multiply physically handicapped, developmentally-disabled individuals to high functioning autistic children and adults, to corporate supervisors, managers, and CEOs. There are perhaps a dozen specialized journals which publish research in the various areas of behavior analysis. The ethical behavior analyst has to keep up with the latest developments in his or her specialty to meet the expectation of "excellence" embodied in the BACB Guidelines.

In addition to the methodology requirement, there is a further commitment to the science in that there must be a scientific basis for the treatment itself. Behavior analysts require of themselves and their profession that practitioners keep up with the research literature and only apply procedures that have first been proven effective in the laboratory or other controlled settings. Furthermore, all modifications in treatment must be based on the online data that is collected as the treatment progresses. Although "evidence-based treatment" has recently become a catch phrase in psychology and medicine, it has been standard procedure in behavior analysis for over thirty years. To be included in the library of possible procedures, a study must meet rigorous peer-review standards of excellence. Perhaps the most rigorous standard is that a clear demonstration of experimental control must be shown; simple correlations need not apply. Behavior analyst practitioners rely on this solid foundation for their treatment ideas and need a good deal of confidence that a given procedure will, in fact, produce a specific outcome. There is some considerable degree of judgment that is required, however, in adapting each procedure to each client. A review of the literature may not reveal an intervention with exactly the population or client characteristics that are being treated at the time, or a treatment may seem appropriate but some features may need to be changed, such as the type of reinforcer or schedule of reinforcement.

Another aspect of treatment that makes behavior analysis unique is that, to a great extent, treatments are carried out by others, often paraprofessionals, under the supervision of a certified professional. For example, Board Certified Behavior Analysts® (BCBAs or CBAs for short) may be working with caregivers, parents, or teachers, for example, in the treatment of a child behavior problem. The CBA is responsible for determining the seriousness of the behavior, establishing baseline data collection, doing the necessary background work, and carrying out a functional assessment. Once the CBA has determined what the controlling variables are, a treatment plan is designed, approved, and put in place. This latter step may involve the behavior analyst demonstrating to the rest of the "team" how a procedure should be carried out and then carefully training them to do so reliably and with precision. The behavior analyst is bound by the ethics code to use this approach; to do less than thorough training, or to allow unqualified persons to use the procedures, would essentially be unethical.

Traditionally, the clinical psychologist carries out therapy in a clinic setting, one-on-one with patients who self-select for treatment. When the session is over, the "patient" leaves the clinic under his or her own steam and drives home or goes to work. With the vast majority of behavior analysis treatment, the work is done in the setting where the behavior problem actually occurs. Our clients are likely to have been referred by someone else for treatment and often the behavior is severe enough that the person must be under some sort of supervision, possibly in a residential setting. This combination of working in real-world settings, with severe behavior problems, certainly makes behavior analysis unique and presents a special set of ethical problems. First, because the person being treated was likely referred by someone else, we need to be especially careful to respect the rights of the client. We need to make sure that the referring person, often referred to as "the third party," has not made the referral for treatment based on mere convenience. It could happen, for example, in a residential setting, that staff members might refer a client for treatment of screaming or running away. The behavior analyst must be careful to respect the rights of the client who was referred because that individual may be yelling and screaming or trying to leave the setting because he or she is being mistreated in some way. To establish a program to simply suppress the screaming or stop the running would be unethical. Second, working in full view of other professionals, staff, and administrators, can present additional ethical dilemmas. Special care must be taken not to stigmatize the client with obtrusive observation systems or methods of data collection, yet the data needs to be reliable and valid. Walking this fine line presents the ethical behavior analyst with challenges every working day. Finally, the behavior analyst is often found working with vulnerable populations who are unable to protect themselves from harm. In contrast to the clinical patient who drives home after a one-hour talk-therapy session, our clients often cannot speak or ambulate. The ethical behavior analyst must do everything possible to make sure that the client's rights are not violated in the process of receiving treatment. A twenty-five-year old developmentally-disabled, nonverbal, nonambulatory individual who engages in SIB still has a right to privacy, a right to be treated with dignity and respect, and a right to effective treatment, for example. The individual cannot simply be restrained, isolated, or overmedicated to stop the behavior. Analyzing the behavior while trying to protect the client's rights is a tall order but is required by our code of ethics. Although in this example the referral involved only a request that a behavior be reduced (SIB), the behavior analyst has an additional requirement to determine how greater independence might be given to the client to possibly prevent future occurrences of the challenging behavior. The aforementioned developmentally-disabled adult may have been screaming because he was in pain, or because he was trying to signal that he was thirsty or needed attention. The ethical behavior analyst is required to carry out a functional assessment to determine such possible causes and to develop appropriate interventions, such as teaching a less dangerous method of signaling staff of his needs. Clearly, an intervention of this nature is more ethically appropriate than the use of a punisher, such as time-out, to reduce the referred behavior of screaming.

Behavior analysts are often called in to work on cases where the behavior is not only quite severe but also amazingly complex in nature. As determinists, we assume that the behavior we see has a causal basis and we believe that doing a functional analysis will help yield information that will produce valid, ethical treatments. However, arriving at the point of treatment involves a myriad of variables that are difficult to access. The SIB alluded to earlier may have had its cause in some medical condition that occurred years earlier (e.g., the client had a chronic sore that went untreated), but the variables that maintain the behavior might be completely different (e.g., staff attention). Other complexities might include the occurrence of conditioned reinforcers or complex schedules of intermittent reinforcement which are operating to maintain the behavior, establishing operations that provide motivation from time to time, or discriminative stimuli and setting events which also set the occasion for the behavior. The ethical behavior analyst must examine all these possibilities and determine which are most salient in arriving at a treatment approach.

One hallmark of behavior analysis from its earliest days remains the role of consequences in modifying behavior. In the beginning, although most other helping professions relied on counseling or "talk therapy" to change attitudes or feelings, "behavior modification" put an emphasis on consequences, often aversive consequences. And, combined with a lack of clear ethical or professional guidelines, there were some tragic results that tarnished the field and gave us a reputation that was difficult to shake. Many of the advances in ethical controls for behavior analysis came out of this era.

Aversive consequences would currently be considered "more restrictive" procedures and would be recommended only after reinforcement procedures had been tried, and if aversive procedures were to be used, the client or his or her surrogate would have to give approval. It is further recommended that if any punishment procedures are used that reinforcement for alternative behaviors is also included in the program. Clearly, ethical behavior analysts have their work cut out for them on the use of consequences. Staying on the side of positive reinforcement must be balanced with the client's right to effective treatment.

One final way that behavior analysis is unique involves the way in which behavior analysts are employed. Currently we are likely to be either working for a state agency or a private consulting firm: the employer is a third party. When the service is paid directly by the patient, presumably there is sufficient countercontrol to prevent abuses, ensure that the service meets the needs of the consumer, and prevent the sort of harm that was seen in the Sunland Miami case. Agencies must be diligent not only in hiring qualified behavior analysts but must also assume responsibility for their actions on a day-to-day basis. Whether state or private, some entity or organization has to keep tabs on their professionals' performance, assume a monitoring function, and exert some form of quality assurance. This can be a tall order when we live in a culture where role models, from college coaches to American presidents, are regularly accused of unethical conduct. In practice, this means that the employer must be fully aware of the Guidelines for Responsible Conduct. The employer must be prepared to keep tabs on the activities of the behavior analysts who are working in the field under very little, if any, supervision. Here again, the responsibility for ethical conduct goes to the behavior analyst who must uphold the highest standards so as not to harm clients or tarnish the reputation of the employer. Not often mentioned is the problem of the employer who may push the behavior analyst to engage in unseemly or possibly unethical behavior. In this instance, the behavior analyst's pledge to support the Guidelines must supersede the desire of the employer to cut corners or increase profits. The myriad of complexities that are encountered when the behavior analyst works for a third party presents perhaps the most difficult challenges of all, because, to deny an employer's request may result in termination. This is clearly a high price to pay for ethical conduct.

The behavior analyst has the potential to do great good for clients and society by analyzing complex problematic behaviors, finding humane and effective solutions, implementing programs that work, and assuring the least-restrictive, most-effective, evidence-based treatments possible given limited resources. It is the goal of the BACB Guidelines to assure that this outcome is consistently achieved while protecting clients' rights at all times.

II

Understanding and Following the Behavior Analyst Certification Board Guidelines for Responsible Conduct in Real-life Contexts

In Part II, chapters 4 through 13 address each of the ten sections of the BACB Guidelines. In these chapters, the actual text of the Guidelines is italicized. Our explanatory "in plain English" comments follow in nonitalics. We developed the cases and they are not a part of the BACB Guidelines. Chapter 14 offers advice to those who are making the transition from student or trainee, considering and performing their first job.

Chapter 4

Responsible Conduct
of a Behavior Analyst (Guideline 1)

As a profession, behavior analysis has evolved in a unique way when compared to the other "helping professions." We have a relatively short history, going back only to the mid-1960s, and our roots are firmly planted in the experimental analysis of behavior. The original behavior analysts were often experimental psychologists who recognized how their animal lab procedures could be applied to help the human condition. The original applications with humans (Ayllon & Michael, 1959; Wolf, Risley, & Mees, 1964) were almost direct replications of experimental (animal lab) procedures. These procedures were used with populations that were abandoned by the other service professionals at the time. This was also a time in which questions about the ethics of treatment were not raised. Well-trained, responsible, experimental psychologists used their own conscience, common sense, and respect for human values to create new treatments. Based on learning theory, it was believed that these treatments might work to relieve suffering or dramatically improve the quality of life for institutionalized individuals who were not receiving any other forms of effective treatment. There were no "guidelines for responsible conduct" and there was no oversight of these PhD researchers turned cutting-edge therapists. Their work was done in the public eye with full knowledge of parents or guardians, and a review of the work today would find little to fault in terms of ethical conduct. It was only much later that some poorly prepared and insensitive behavior analysts would run into ethical problems creating the scandals described in chapter 1.

Today, as a field, we have very high expectations for practicing behavior analysts, and Guideline 1.0 addresses this concern for overall responsible conduct. This Guideline expresses the value system of our field which states that those professionals who want to call themselves behavior analysts must conduct themselves in a way that reflects positively on the field—very positively in fact. Guideline 1.01 emphasizes our roots in the science of behavior (Skinner, 1953) and reminds behavior analysts that the decisions they make from day to day must be tied to this science. This is actually a very tall order given the thousands of applied behavioral studies that have been conducted in the last forty years. Currently, there are nearly two dozen journals worldwide which publish behavioral research (American Psychological Association, 2001), so the ethical behavior analyst has an obligation to keep in touch with quite a bit of "scientific knowledge." Another expectation is that the behavior analyst remain "proficient in professional practice." This is another demanding standard given the constantly improving methodology of our relatively young field. In the early years of behavior analysis, there was an emphasis on the use of aversive procedures to change behavior, which unfortunately set the stage for considerable backlash on the part of advocate and consumer groups. An "anti-aversives" movement began and still exists that has portrayed our field as prone to the use of punishment although we have long since passed into another level of professionalism. As happens in many fields, some practitioners seem to become frozen in time with regard to their skills. It is possible even now to run into someone who got a PhD in 1975 who has not remained current with the trends in the field. This Guideline was meant as a wake-up call to such individuals for them to get back in touch with current standards before they hurt innocent people and damage the reputations of legitimate, up-to-date behavior analysts.

It does not seem too much to ask of any professional that he or she recognize the legal code of his or her community and maintain high moral principles. To do otherwise is to put a stain on the good reputation of others. Even although not practicing behavior analysis, the community will identify you as a member of that group if something goes amiss. None of us wants to see a headline like, "Behavior analyst caught dealing drugs at local high school," but that is exactly how a headline would read. As a new profession with a complex two-part name, we are not on the radar screens of most Americans. Our goal is to gradually emerge onto the scene with a terrific reputation for truth, honesty, and reliability. What we don't want is to end up on the "Ten Least Respected Professions" list along with journalists and government employees (BBC Radio, 1999). So, our admonition to those entering behavior analysis is to monitor your own behavior, make sure that, in your dealings with your clients and the public, your conduct is above reproach, well within the law, and that you would be recognized by those around you as an exemplary citizen.

When the behavior analyst is operating professionally, others are observing and making judgments about his or her conduct. Is the behavior analyst forthright and honest or somewhat devious and deceptive? Does he or she talk down to her professional colleagues or treat them with respect? Does he or she demean the work of others or attempt to collaborate and educate? If we are to advance our field, we must, as a new profession, gain the respect of all those we work with by our "responsible conduct" every day and many aspects of this behavior are discussed in Guideline 1.06. We discourage all behavior analysts from becoming "shade tree mechanics" (Guideline 1.06a) and to translate their suggested treatment plan into plain English for clients, consumers, and other professionals (1.06b), saving the jargon for behavioral colleagues at conferences.

A major personal commitment that we ask of behavior analysts is to shed and ultimately reject any biases they may have grown up with in their families or communities and learn to deal with people of different genders, race, ethnicity, or national origin in a totally accepting and nondiscriminating manner. It is unacceptable that a behavior analyst would treat a person of a different race or socioeconomic status any differently than he or she would someone of his or her own race or status.

This may be quite a stretch for some newcomers to our field and it could present major challenges, depending on your commitment to another value system (strength of your conditioning history). If you are a graduate student and see any problems related to your values, now is the time to reflect on your situation and approach one of your professors for a frank talk about this issue and the implications for your future success in the field.

Sexual harassment is a blight on our culture that will not go away. Over 13,000 charges are filed each year, 85% of which are made by women, and with fines reaching $50 million each year to resolve the conflicts (U.S. Equal Employment Opportunity Commission, 2004). Sexual harassment is a form of sex discrimination that violates Title VII of the Civil Rights Act of 1964. One would think that most professionals would be aware of this. However, even attorneys have engaged in this despicable form of abuse as noted in the case of Anita Hill in her testimony against Clarence Thomas (Hill, 1998). This form of conduct includes unwelcome advances, requests for sexual favors, and any form of behavior that is sufficiently severe and pervasive and produces an abusive working environment (Binder, 1992).

Even behavior analysts may develop problems in their personal lives. Chronic illness, a messy divorce, or alcohol addiction can bring most anyone down, and, as in the case of any professional, your obligation is to make sure that personal issues do not interfere with your ability to deliver quality services (Guideline 1.06f). This is probably best handled via the "trusted colleague" model described in chapter 1 in which you develop a relationship with a person on whom you can rely to be straight and honest with you on a range of matters that affect your professional life. If you in any way feel that you might not be fulfilling your obligations to your clients or in your workplace, it is time to have a heart-to-heart talk with this colleague to determine his or her perceptions and help you sort out your options. Some of those will probably involve taking a leave of absence for a period of time while you get your life back in order. During this time, you need to make sure that you have made arrangements with other behavior analysts to cover your clients and sit for you on committees.

Effective behavior analysts wear many hats in their community and it is easy for them to encounter situations where some conflict of interest might arise (Guideline 1.07). Such conflicts come about because the busy, effective behavior analyst who has a full client caseload might also have other responsibilities such as serving on the peer review committee, being an elected representative of his or her state association, and possibly having some responsibility with his or her local Parent Teacher Organization (PTO). More personal conflicts of interest can arise when a neighbor asks for help with a child behavior problem or a visiting relative clearly needs help resolving a personal issue. A behavior analyst who is a government employee, elected to a position with a state organization, may find that the position the organization takes on an issue is at odds with his or her employer; a behavior analyst who freely gives advice to a relative runs the risk of alienating that person if the program goes bad or his or her advice is contrary to what the school psychologist or counselor recommended. The best solution is to avoid such situations on the front end but the Guidelines require the behavior analyst to resolve them before any harm is done (Guideline 1.07c).

As our profession has grown over the past 40 years, behavior analysts have increasingly been respected for their skills and have moved into positions of authority where they wield some considerable power and influence. Whereas in the beginning they served only as therapists or unit directors, many behavior analysts are now chairpersons of psychology departments, superintendents of large residential facilities, or owners of major consulting firms. In such positions, even the most ethically sensitive behavior analyst may find that he or she can call the shots without anyone else's approval. The PhD president of a consulting firm can direct his or her master's-degree-level consultants to advocate a certain procedure, promote overbilling, or encourage snooping on the competition while on the job. We would hope that the ethical master's-level consultant would resist such pressure but the differential in power allows supervisees to be exploited if care is not taken. Supervisors could extract favors from students in exchange for a good grade in practicum, and theoretically, behavioral faculty could do the same. Or, as has occasionally been reported, students may offer favors for a good grade. Thus, parties on both sides need to be equally aware of the potential for exploitation when one person is in control, even if the person is a behavior analyst.

RESPONSIBLE CONDUCT OF A BEHAVIOR ANALYST (GUIDELINE 1.0)

The behavior analyst maintains the high standards of professional behavior of the professional organization.

Professional behavior here is distinguished from private or everyday behavior. This means that when you are at work or serving on a committee where you are representing your profession or organization, you must uphold the standards expected by the profession. These are understood to include honesty, integrity, reliability, confidentiality, and trustworthiness.

CASE EXAMPLE AND QUESTION 14:
DR. ELAINE J. AND JANE P.

Jane P., a CABA who serves on a state association nominating committee, very much wants her colleague Dr. Elaine J. to be elected. Jane begins by talking to the CBAs she knows and tells them that Dr. J. is absolutely the best person for the job. Jane realizes she will gain influence on the Board if her friend, Dr. J., is elected.

Why are there ethical problems associated with Jane's political strategy?

RELIANCE ON SCIENTIFIC KNOWLEDGE (1.01)

Behavior analysts rely on scientifically and professionally derived knowledge when making scientific or professional judgments in human service provision, or when engaging in scholarly or professional endeavors.

One of the characteristics of behavior analysis that makes it unique is the reliance on scientific evidence as a basis for our practice. As a general rule, we expect to base our methods of assessment on systematic observation of behavior and one of several methods of functional assessment. Although we might seek input from family or care-givers during an intake process, the behavior analyst depends on objective data that is sufficient to allow some conclusion. This same data collection system is used along with treatment data to determine if a change in behavior has occurred. When presenting findings at a conference or for publication, it is essential that you maintain the highest standards of integrity for description of your method and results that you obtained.

COMPETENCE AND PROFESSIONAL DEVELOPMENT (1.02)

The behavior analyst remains proficient in professional practice and the performance of professional functions by reading the appropriate literature, attending conferences and conventions, participating in workshops, and/or obtaining Behavior Analyst Certification Board certification.

Behavior analysis is a rapidly growing field and it is necessary to remain in close touch with all new developments. This means attending your state association conference as well as the annual meeting of the Association for Behavior Analysis as a critical part of your professional commitment. You should also subscribe to the most important journals in the field and review those articles relevant to your practice or area of research.

CASE EXAMPLE AND QUESTION 15: DR. JERRY J.

Jerry J., a CBA with a heart condition, finds that he is unable to attend the annual meeting of ABA. He wants to keep up with the field but has been advised by his doctor against plane travel.

Are there any alternatives other than traveling a long distance for Dr. J.?

COMPETENCE (1.03)

(a) Behavior analysts provide services, teach, and conduct research only within the boundaries of their competence, based on their education, training, supervised experience, or appropriate professional experience.

Boundaries of competence in behavior analysis are sometimes difficult to discern. However, you are obligated to practice only in those areas where you have had formal training.

CASE EXAMPLE AND QUESTION 16: DR. SANDRA F.

Dr. Sandra F., a professor at a small midwestern college, is asked to teach a course in child psychology. Dr. F. is a CBA with a PhD from a major university and although she did her dissertation on children with phobias, she has never taken a graduate course or seminar specifically on this topic.

How should Dr. F. handle this request?

(b) Behavior analysts provide services, teach, or conduct research in new areas or involving new techniques only after first undertaking appropriate study, training, supervision, and/or consultation from persons who are competent in those areas or techniques.

When you feel it is necessary to practice outside the areas in which you were trained, you are required to seek further training in the new area.

PROFESSIONAL DEVELOPMENT (1.04)

Behavior analysts who engage in assessment, therapy, teaching, research, organizational consulting, or other professional activities maintain a reasonable level of awareness of current scientific and professional informa-

tion in their fields of activity, and undertake ongoing efforts to maintain competence in the skills they use.

As a behavior analyst, you are required to stay current in your specialty area. This means you should subscribe to and read the relevant journals in your specialty and attend conferences and workshops that are specific to your area of practice, research, or therapy.

CASE EXAMPLE AND QUESTION 17: TONY H.

Tony H., a CBA chair of a local behavioral review committee, has noticed that in the last several meetings, one of the presenters is very much behind on current behavioral treatment. The presenter, also a CBA, has many years experience and is well thought of in the community. Other committee members have begun to make occasional embarrassing comments about this person behind his back at the end of the meetings.

What are some suggestions for how Tony could handle this situation in a professional and tactful manner?

INTEGRITY (1.05)

(a) The behavior analyst's behavior conforms to the legal and moral codes of the social and professional community of which the behavior analyst is a member.

You are required to be aware of legal issues pertaining to the delivery of services in your state and you need to be cognizant of moral and social values in your community. Although behavioral procedures have been shown to work in a vast array of circumstances and settings, it is only because the behavior analyst gained the confidence of key members of the community and worked within the informal social codes of conduct that were prescribed by the professional community.

CASE EXAMPLE AND QUESTION 18: DR. J.

Dr. J. recently was recruited to teach at a major university where he was expected to set up a laboratory to study self-injurious behavior. His previous research emphasized the effectiveness of certain aversive stimuli which, when made contingent on early responses in the SIB chain, greatly reduced the probability of the final members of the chain being emitted. The work had been published in prestigious journals. Dr. J. was shocked when one of the CABAs he hired to work in the lab said that this research was prohibited by a state law that had been passed about 10 years before.

What corrective steps does Dr. J. need to take now?

(b) The activity of a behavior analyst falls under these Guidelines only if the activity is part of his or her work-related functions or the activity is behavior analytic in nature.

These guidelines cover your activities when you are at work and when you are engaged in other activities that involve basic principles of behavior.

(c) If behavior analysts' ethical responsibilities conflict with law, behavior analysts make known their commitment to these Guidelines and take steps to resolve the conflict in a responsible manner in accordance with law.

If you find yourself in a situation where it appears there is a conflict between these Guidelines and some state statute, you will need to resolve the issue without breaking the law. The most common example of a law that ethical behavior analysts may feel the need to question would be a state law pertaining to confidentiality. In some cases, the behavior analyst may feel conflicted if the client's safety is at risk and someone needs to be told.

PROFESSIONAL AND SCIENTIFIC RELATIONSHIPS (1.06)

(a) Behavior analysts provide behavioral diagnostic, therapeutic, teaching, research, supervisory, consultative, or other behavior analytic services only in the context of a defined, remunerated professional or scientific relationship or role.

You should not "volunteer" to treat someone without some authority to do so. If you do pro bono work for a family or an agency, your role and responsibility must be clearly specified. They must be informed of your credentials and competence. It is recommended that you have something in writing to document this relationship.

(b) When behavior analysts provide assessment, evaluation, treatment, counseling, supervision, teaching, consultation, research, or other behavior analytic services to an individual, a group, or an organization, they use language that is fully understandable to the recipient of those services. They provide appropriate information prior to service delivery about the nature of such services and appropriate information later about results and conclusions.

When you are working with lay people, speak English and be diligent in making sure they understand what you are doing both prior to intervention and in follow-up.

CASE EXAMPLE AND QUESTION 19: MATTHEW T.

Matthew T. was a CABA who just recently graduated from college and was taking his first job as a behavior analyst. He wanted to impress his clients with his newfound knowledge and so sprinkled terms like tact, mand, autoclitic, and control procedures liberally in his meetings with parents. His supervisor received complaints from the parents saying, "We have no idea what he is talking about but it sounds scary to us."

What should the supervisor do about this CABA and his technical way of talking about things?

(c) Where differences of age, gender, race, ethnicity, national origin, religion, sexual orientation, disability, language, or socioeconomic status significantly affect behavior analysts' work concerning particular individuals or groups, behavior analysts obtain the training, experience, consultation, or supervision necessary to ensure the competence of their services, or they make appropriate referrals.

If you are working with individuals different from those to whom you are accustomed, you should seek guidance from another professional. Alternatively, you may consider referring the clients to another behavior analyst.

(d) In their work-related activities, behavior analysts do not engage in discrimination against individuals or groups based on age, gender, race, ethnicity, national origin, religion, sexual orientation, disability, socioeconomic status, or any basis proscribed by law.

It is unethical to discriminate against others in your work-related activities for any reason. You may not treat people unfairly or provide less or unsatisfactory treatment just because they are different from you.

CASE EXAMPLE AND QUESTION 20: AHMED

Ahmed had always been fascinated by psychology and took a special undergraduate track that prepared him to sit for the Associates test offered by the BACB. He earned good grades and excelled at doing descriptive functional assessments in his practicum. When he got his first job, he discovered that one of his student clients in an elementary school was a Sunni Muslim. Ahmed men-

tioned this to his parents who were irate and insisted that he refuse to associate in any way with this student of a rival religious sect.

Ahmed is in a very sensitive situation. How should he handle this?

(e) Behavior analysts do not knowingly engage in behavior that is harassing or demeaning to persons with whom they interact in their work based on factors such as those persons' age, gender, race, ethnicity, national origin, religion, sexual orientation, disability, language, or socioeconomic, status in accordance with law.

As a behavior analyst, you should be sensitive to the reaction others have to your behavior. It is inappropriate to make sexual advances to others ("flirting"), to tease or make demeaning comments about their size, weight, sexual orientation, age, or any other noticeable feature.

(f) Behavior analysts recognize that their personal problems and conflicts may interfere with their effectiveness. Behavior analysts refrain from providing services when their personal circumstances may compromise delivering services to the best of their abilities.

As a behavior analyst, you have an obligation to monitor your own behavior and recognize when stress, changes in life situation (e.g., death in the family, divorce), or some conflict negatively affect your professional performance. In such cases, you will need to make arrangements for another behavior analyst to serve your clients until you recover.

CASE EXAMPLE AND QUESTION 21: STELLA V.

A forty-something CBA, Stella V. came home after a long day of analyzing behavior to discover that her husband had left her. His note said he was unhappy with never seeing his wife, that she had

*changed since their marriage ten years earlier, and that he was go-
ing on a "voyage of self-exploration." Although she denied to everyone that it bothered her, Stella's work became erratic and she
appeared to be unusually prickly about feedback on her functional
assessments. She walked out in the middle of one parent meeting
saying, "I just can't take this any more." Stella's colleagues were
worried about her and they were very concerned about her recent
performance.*

Should the behavioral colleagues get involved in Stella's personal
business?

DUAL RELATIONSHIPS (1.07)

*(a) In many communities and situations, it may not be feasible or reason-
able for behavior analysts to avoid social or other nonprofessional contacts
with persons such as clients, students, supervisees, or research participants.
Behavior analysts must always be sensitive to the potential harmful effects
of other contacts on their work and on those persons with whom they deal.*

You should strive to avoid social contacts with your clients because
it might interfere with your objectivity as a behavior analyst or possibly harm or exploit them. With supervisees, students, or research participants, it is also a good idea to avoid any more than casual contact
as this might be construed as showing favoritism in the case of students or supervisees or bias their participation in the case of research
participants.

CASE EXAMPLE AND QUESTION 22

*A CBA who lives in a small town was asked by her sister to develop
an ABA program for her son. There are no other behavior analysts
available and the CBA has issues with the sister that would be
complicated by her taking the case.*

What is the CBA's most appropriate course of action?

(b) A behavior analyst refrains from entering into or promising a personal, scientific, professional, financial, or other relationship with any such person if it appears likely that such a relationship reasonably might impair the behavior analyst's objectivity or otherwise interfere with the behavior analyst's ability to effectively perform his or her functions as a behavior analyst, or might harm or exploit the other party.

It is best to avoid dual relationships with others (e.g., student and business associate) if it appears that this will negatively affect your ability to be effective as a behavior analyst or might in some way harm the other person.

(c) If a behavior analyst finds that, due to unforeseen factors, a potentially harmful multiple relationship has arisen (i.e., one in which the reasonable possibility of conflict of interest or undue influence is present), the behavior analyst attempts to resolve it with due regard for the best interests of the affected person and maximal compliance with these Guidelines.

If you find that you have become involved in a harmful dual relationship with a client or other professional, you are required to resolve the situation in the best interests of the person and with due regard for these Guidelines.

EXPLOITATIVE RELATIONSHIPS (1.08)

(a) Behavior analysts do not exploit persons over whom they have supervisory, evaluative, or other authority such as students, supervisees, employees, research participants, and clients.

Behavior analysts do not use or take advantage of anyone regardless of whether the behavior analysts supervise them or have some sort of authority over them.

(b) Behavior analysts do not engage in sexual relationships with clients, students, or supervisees in training over whom the behavior analyst has evaluative or direct authority, because such relationships easily impair judgment or become exploitative.

Do not become involved in sexual relationships with clients, students, or supervisees because such relationships can impair your judgment. Also, you may be exploited or find that you are taken advantage of by the other party.

CASE EXAMPLE AND QUESTION 23: BILL Q. AND KRISTI

Bill Q. was a thirty-year-old, single BCBA who worked with clients and conducted research in a large state institution. Bill had a good working relationship with the local university's psychology and special education programs. One semester, Bill found himself attracted to Kristi, one of the college students he was supervising. The attraction seemed mutual because Kristi made it a point to let Bill know that she was single and available for dating.

Because the feelings seemed to be mutual, was there any problem with Bill asking Kristi for a date?

(c) Behavior analysts are cautioned against bartering with clients because it is often (1) clinically contraindicated, and (2) prone to formation of an exploitative relationship.

Bartering is the exchange of goods or services in lieu of payment. It is strongly discouraged because it can easily go awry when one party feels that he or she has not received an equal return according to the agreement.

CASE EXAMPLE AND QUESTION 24:
JULIE S., ROSITA, AND MANNY G.

Julie S. was a CBA who provided behavioral services to families and their children. Julie was working in the home with two of the children of Rosita and Manny G.

Rosita and Manny were the owners of a very popular Mexican restaurant. On one visit, Rosita suggested to Julie that instead of paying for behavioral services with a check, she and Manny would like to trade out food at their restaurant.

Julie was a fan of Rosita's tamales and as long as she kept a close watch on her hours of service versus visits to the restaurant, would this mutually agreed on system be within the Guidelines?

RESPONSES TO CASE QUESTION 14:
DR. ELAINE J. AND JANE P.

Jane is in violation of 1.0 of the Guidelines; she is not maintaining high standards for professional behavior. She is trying to influence her friends to vote for someone for her own gain. She has a hidden agenda and she is not being honest. As a Board member, she is also violating her role as a person who is supposed to be objective and impartial. She should not be trying to influence the way that other CBAs vote if she is on the Board.

RESPONSES TO CASE QUESTION 15: DR. JERRY J.

The behavior analyst, who very much wants to maintain his status as a cutting-edge professional, finds that he can purchase tapes of "Tutorials" presented at ABA and that by closely reviewing the programs, he can find important new topics on which he needs to remain current. He determines that for the cost of the trip to ABA, he can purchase the tapes and subscribe

to two additional journals in his specialty area. (Tutorials are presenta-
tions on videotape by the country's leading ABA experts. They are available
in a variety of topics, such as performance management and autism. They
are available through the online store of Association for Behavior Analy-
sis.) Additionally, behavior analysts should check to see if there is an active
state association which they can join. This is a relatively easy way to earn
continuing education credits without having to travel a great distance.

RESPONSES TO CASE QUESTION 16: DR. SANDRA F.

The professor meets with the chairperson of the department to explain that
she would be reluctant to teach the course because she has not had formal
training in this area and that the BACB Code requires that behavior ana-
lysts operate within their "boundaries of competence." The professor sug-
gests the course be called "Behavior Analysis and Therapy with Children."
This suggestion was approved by the department chairperson.

RESPONSES TO CASE QUESTION 17: TONY H.

Tony asks the CBA to stay after one of the meetings and begins a low-key
conversation about a speaker he heard at a recent conference that he at-
tended, looking for some sign of recognition or interest. When this was not
forthcoming, he became a little bolder, asking that the CBA consider look-
ing into some recent articles on behavioral treatment that seemed quite rel-
evant. Again, seeing no sign of interest, Tony said, "I'm concerned about
your clients, I'm not sure they are getting the best treatment available."
Tony H. is professional and tactful as he points out the 1.02 standard in the
BACB Guidelines.

RESPONSES TO CASE QUESTION 18: DR. J.

In some states, the "use of noxious and painful stimuli" is not allowed in the
treatment of developmentally-disabled individuals or others who receive ser-

vices from state agencies. Dr. J. was required to change the focus of his treatment to a different type of question regarding the use of NCR (noncontingent reinforcement), a topic in which he also had a strong interest.

RESPONSES TO CASE QUESTION 19: MATTHEW T.

The supervisor met with the CABA and reminded him about translating his technical terminology into closely equivalent English words. He gave the CABA a list of common terms that could be interchanged with behavioral terminology and urged him to practice using them. After the next meeting, the supervisor checked with the family to see if they felt any more comfortable with the CABA.

RESPONSES TO CASE QUESTION 20: AHMED

Refusing to provide treatment of a person based on religion, ethnicity, or national origin is considered a form of discrimination and is not condoned by the BACB Guidelines and is illegal as well. This means Ahmed cannot discriminate against the child and refuse treatment just to satisfy his parents. If he cannot be totally unbiased, he must make a referral to another CBA (1.06c & 1.06f). In addition, Ahmed needs to rethink his commitment to his chosen field.

RESPONSES TO CASE QUESTION 21: STELLA V.

Although specifically trained as behavioral observers, behavior analysts may still not be able to put their own behavior in perspective and see how it affects others. Someone close to Stella needs to take her aside and offer her some assistance. Ideally, this would be a colleague but might also be her supervisor. The main point of this ethical problem is that you have an obligation to talk to a colleague whose performance is not up to standard. In this case, the supervisor might suggest a leave of absence for Stella to give her a chance to focus on getting her life under control.

RESPONSES TO CASE QUESTION 22

The CBA decides not to take the case and contacts her state association to lo-cate someone who would be willing to work with her sister. She also contacts the local school system to determine if there are services available there. If this is, for example, a very rural area where there is absolutely no one else who can provide behavioral services, it may be necessary for a non-CBA to work with the child. The CBA may wish to begin training other profession-als on behavioral skills (e.g., a talented teacher) and it might be possible that someone else could work with the family.

RESPONSES TO CASE QUESTION 23: BILL Q. AND KRISTI

Behavior analysts do not engage in sexual relationships with clients, stu-dents, or supervisees; such a relationship could impair their judgement and constitute a form of exploitation as well. Dating is also in this category. If Bill believes Kristi is the woman of his dreams, he should wait until her in-ternship is over to have nonprofessional contact with her. Depending on the nature of the interactions, it might be appropriate to find someone else to supervise Kristi.

RESPONSES TO CASE QUESTION 24:
JULIE S., ROSITA, AND MANNY G.

The Guidelines caution behavior analysts against bartering because it is of-ten clinically contraindicated and it can result in the forming of exploit-ative relationships. The potential for a perceived imbalance or unfairness by either party is also great. If Rosita and Manny feel that the therapy is not going well, and that progress is slow with their children, they may provide less stellar service to Julie in their restaurant. Julie, on the other hand, may feel that the extra hours she puts in should be worth an extra margarita now and then. The possibilities are endless for squabbling and such an arrange-ment has little to do with Julie providing quality behavioral services.

Chapter 5

The Behavior Analyst's Responsibility to Clients (Guideline 2)

In the early days, when our field consisted of experimental psychologists applying the principles of behavior to "subjects" they encountered on the residential units of institutions, there was no question about where the responsibility lay; it was clearly with the employer. These pioneer behavior analysts most often had no training in clinical psychology. They believed that behavior could be changed using procedures derived from learning theory. The "client" (although that term was not used initially) was their employer. In some cases, the parents of a child were the "clients."

It wasn't until 1974 that issues of a client's "right to treatment" would surface as an issue in the landmark *Wyatt v. Stickney* (1971) case in Alabama. In this case, it was argued that institutionalized mental patients had a right to receive individual treatment or be discharged to the community. Although the case really did not have anything directly to do with treatment per se (it dictated increases in professional staff, improvements in the physical plant, and how many showers a patient should receive per week, for example), it blasted the term *right to treatment* into the legal arena and put all psychologists, including behavior analysts, on notice that a paradigm shift had occurred. In behavior analysis, we immediately became sensitive to the possibility that our "client" might be harmed by our procedures and in a short period of time, "clients' rights" were the new watchwords. The original trial judge, Frank M. Johnson, Jr., set forth what later became known as the "Wyatt Standards." This case was precedent-setting and put all mental health and retardation professionals on notice that their services had to be delivered in humane environments, where there were sufficient qualified staff, individualized treatment plans, and that the treatment had to be delivered in the least restrictive environment. Following the Wyatt decision, if you were assigned to work with a client in a residential facility, it was clear that you had an obligation not only to the facility to do your best work but a responsibility to the person on the receiving end of the treatment to make sure he or she was not harmed. There was concern in the beginning that "behavioral specialists" (they were not yet called behavior analysts) would manipulate "client" behavior just for the convenience of the staff, for example, punish those clients who were incontinent so that staff members would not have to change their diapers. Over time it became clear that, ethically speaking, it was only right to consider the needs of the actual client along with anyone else who might be affected by the procedures (staff, parents or guardian, other residents, etc.). This immediately made the behavior specialist job far more difficult. By the end of the 1970s, behavior analysis was becoming more widespread and visible and behavior analysts found themselves working with other professionals on "habilitation teams" to determine the right treatment for clients. Thus, the beginning of issues concerning consultation and cooperation with other professionals arose. In addition, there began to be differentiation of the roles of the entities and concerns developed about "third party" involvement. If a client (first party) hires a behavior analyst (second party), presumably there is no conflict of interest and the client can fire the behavior analyst if he or she is not satisfied with the services; likewise, the behavior analyst will do his or her best to satisfy the client's needs so that the behavior analyst will be paid for his or her services. This arrangement has built in checks and balances. But, if the behavior analyst is hired by a third party (e.g., a facility) to treat the behavior of one of its residents (first party), there is a presumption that the behavior analyst will work to satisfy the needs of the third party to keep his or her job. The Guidelines address this issue in some detail in 2.04.

By the 1980s, behavior analysis was much more visible in mental retardation treatment circles and was accepted by many as a viable strategy for habilitation. It was around this time that the further trappings of service delivery had to be accommodated. It was clear that clients had rights (both under the U.S. Constitution and the Wyatt standards) and that everyone, including the behavior analyst, had to respect them, and certainly be informed of them prior to treatment. Furthermore, with behavior analysis approaching the mainstream of accepted approaches, other protections had to be put in place. Clients had a right to privacy and arrangements had to be made to protect their privacy and confidentiality. Records had to be stored and transferred in a way that maintained these rights and behavior analysts had the same obligation as other professionals to obtain consent to disclose the information. By the late 1980s, the time had come for behavior analysts to speak out on the issue of right to treatment and the ABA convened a blue-ribbon panel of experts to reach some consensus on the topic. A consensus was reached and ultimately approved by the governing body of ABA, which essentially stated that clients had a right to a "therapeutic environment" where their personal welfare would be of paramount importance and where they had a right to treatment by a "competent behavior analyst" who would conduct a behavioral assessment, teach functional skills, and evaluate the treatments. The ABA panel finally concluded that clients had a right to "the most effective treatments available" (Van Houten et al., 1988). This reference to effective treatments set the stage for behavior analysts to redouble their efforts to make a direct connection between the published research and the application of empirically tested interventions.

Guideline 2.0 provides a clear and detailed list of the obligations that behavior analysts have if they undertake to treat any client using behavioral procedures. By accepting these responsibilities and taking them seriously, we can guarantee that our clients will receive the first-class treatment they deserve and that as a profession we will have demonstrated our respect for their rights even as we provide state-of-the-art behavioral interventions.

THE BEHAVIOR ANALYST'S RESPONSIBILITY TO CLIENTS (2.0)

The behavior analyst has a responsibility to operate in the best interest of clients.

Although this may seem a truism, it is nonetheless a bedrock value of behavior analysis. As a service provider, you will make many decisions each day that will affect the quality of the treatment you provide. You could decide to cut short a discrete-trial language session so that you can make it to the dry cleaners before it closes, or more significantly, decide to drop a client just because it is somewhat inconvenient to get to his or her house when the traffic is bad. By always asking yourself, "What IS in the best interest of my client?" you will make better decisions in the long run.

DEFINITION OF CLIENT (2.01)

The term client as used here is broadly applicable to whomever the behavior analyst provides services whether an individual person (service recipient), parent or guardian of a service recipient, an institutional representative, a public or private agency, a firm or corporation.

Your client is the person or agency for whom you are providing services. Clients may be individuals, parents, agencies such as schools and Developmental Disability (DD) facilities, or businesses.

RESPONSIBILITY (2.02)

The behavior analyst's responsibility is to all parties affected by behavioral services.

In addition to the client, you are responsible to others who might also be affected by your services. For example, if a school retains you to work with a behaviorally-disordered second grader, you have an obligation to make sure that all principles of ethics extend to the child, the parents, and even other children in the second-grader's classroom.

CASE EXAMPLE AND QUESTION 25: TERRY

Terry was a CBA providing behavioral services to an elementary school student who was aggressive at school and at home. The principal felt a need to put a behavior plan in place immediately because one child had recently been injured by this student. Terry complied with this request. The school social worker offered to explain the program to the parents when they came to the next Parents' Night.

It would be easier for Terry if the social worker talked to the parents instead of him, because he is quite busy right now, but is it okay?

CONSULTATION (2.03)

(a) Behavior analysts arrange for appropriate consultations and referrals based principally on the best interests of their clients, with appropriate consent, and subject to other relevant considerations, including applicable law and contractual obligations.

If the behavior problem you are working on exceeds your level of competence or needs help in an area in which you are not trained, you should seek assistance (consultation from another professional) or make a referral (pass the case to another behavior analyst). This must be done with your client's full knowledge. When considering making a referral to another professional, you must take the client's needs and interests into account. Be careful about referring to your friends as this could violate the prohibition of conflict of interest.

(b) When indicated and professionally appropriate, behavior analysts cooperate with other professionals in order to serve their clients effectively and appropriately. Behavior analysts recognize that other professions

have ethical codes that may differ in their specific requirements from these Guidelines.

You will find that it is often necessary to cooperate with nonbehavioral professionals to meet your client's needs. When interacting with a nonbehavioral professional about one of your clients, keep in mind that other professionals have their own ethical guidelines that may differ from the BACB Guidelines that you need to follow.

CASE EXAMPLE AND QUESTION 26:
DR. ROBERT M. AND JERRY

Dr. Robert M., a BCBA, was providing behavioral services to Jerry, a sixteen-year-old who was disruptive at school. Dr. M. had been working in the field of behavior analysis for twenty years and was very well read in other forms of treatment and psychology. During several of Dr. M.'s visits, Jerry began to talk about issues related to sex. Jerry was clearly confused and troubled about these intimate issues. Dr. M. decided to set some time aside to teach Jerry to "verbalize" his sex-related issues.

Is this acceptable as long as Dr. M. documents this work and does not refer to it as behavior analysis?

THIRD-PARTY REQUESTS FOR SERVICES (2.04)

(a) When a behavior analyst agrees to provide services to a person or entity at the request of a third party, the behavior analyst clarifies to the extent feasible, at the outset of the service, the nature of the relationship with each party. This clarification includes the role of the behavior analyst (such as therapist, organizational consultant, or expert witness), the probable uses of the services provided or the information obtained, and the fact that there may be limits to confidentiality.

If you are asked by a third party (e.g., school system) to treat a child client, for example, you must clarify your relationship to the child, the parent, the teacher, and the school. You must explain your role (e.g., therapist, trainer, consultant, etc.), how you think the information you provide can be used, and remind each one of issues of confidentiality. In a case involving the school, parents, and a child, the parent must give consent for the child to be observed by the behavior analyst on the school grounds and in the classroom. The parent must also give consent for the teacher to see the data. If anyone else requests information on the case, such as the school counselor, the parent must give consent for this too.

(b) If there is a foreseeable risk of the behavior analyst being called upon to perform conflicting roles because of the involvement of a third party, the behavior analyst clarifies the nature and direction of his or her responsibilities, keeps all parties appropriately informed as matters develop, and resolves the situation in accordance with these Guidelines.

If there is some chance that you will be called on to perform a service for the third party (e.g., testify at a hearing), you must clarify this with the second party at the outset of the consultation. If a conflict arises, you must resolve the situation according to the BACB Guidelines.

CASE EXAMPLE AND QUESTION 27: DR. B.

Dr. B. was hired as an organizational consultant by a state Department of Developmental Disabilities. He was assigned to an older, large residential facility for children and adults with developmental disabilities. His job was to help staff develop behavior programs for clients and to provide facility-wide program consultation. Some of the staff thought that Dr. B. was simply a new behavior analyst who was working with clients. They were unaware of the connection with the state and as a result, they were often observed by Dr. B. to be off-task and not working to serve clients.

The administrators knew, of course, that Dr. B. was sent by the state office. As time went on, the facility administrator began to pressure Dr. B. to not report facility problems to the Department of Developmental Disabilities.

What are some procedures Dr. B could implement to manage this situation?

RIGHTS AND PREROGATIVES OF CLIENTS (2.05)

(a) The behavior analyst supports individual rights under the law.

As a behavior analyst, you must support constitutional rights of your clients. In some states, client rights have become expanded to include additional rights to certain kinds of treatment, to hold and keep possessions, to sexual activities, and so on. It is important to explore this issue for each state where you practice.

(b) The client must be provided on request an accurate, current set of the behavior analyst's credentials.

If your client wants to know about your background and training, you should be eager to share an updated vita. This document should be a straightforward, honest, and accurate portrayal of your experience and training. Embellishment is not allowed.

(c) Permission for electronic recording of interviews is secured from clients and all other settings. Consent for different uses must be obtained specifically and separately.

If you find that you need to make audio or video electronic recordings of interviews or behavioral observations, you must get permission from each client individually. If you plan to use the recordings for some purpose other than therapy, you must obtain permission each time to use the recordings.

(d) Clients must be informed of their rights, and about procedures to complain about professional practices of the behavior analyst.

Your clients should be told of their rights to confidentiality. They should also be advised they have the right to withdraw from treatment or a research project at any time. Additionally, you must inform clients about how to voice any complaints regarding your services to your supervisor or to the BACB.

CASE EXAMPLE AND QUESTION 28: SUSAN P. AND SARA

Susan P. was a graduate student working as a behavior specialist. Susan planned to do her doctoral dissertation on adolescents who were physically abused. By coincidence, Susan was assigned to work with Sara, an interesting, verbal, fourteen-year-old, who was more than happy to describe her history of abuse for anyone who would listen. Susan decided to videotape an interview with Sara and one year later, she used this tape as part of a local conference presentation. As it turned out, one of the people in the audience knew Sara's mother. The friend told the mother the video had been shown and the mother was extremely upset. She called Susan in a fury. Susan explained to the mother that this was an acceptable practice because she did not reveal Sara's last name or the name of her parents in the presentation.

If the identify of clients is protected (i.e., their names are not used), is it acceptable to present their cases, videotapes, audiotapes, and so forth?

MAINTAINING CONFIDENTIALITY (2.06)

(a) Behavior analysts have a primary obligation and take reasonable precautions to respect the confidentiality of those with whom they work or con-

sult, recognizing that confidentiality may be established by law, institutional rules, or professional or scientific relationships.

It is very important that you respect and protect the confidentiality of your clients. You may not talk about or share data with regard to your clients with anyone without their explicit consent. You are responsible for understanding the law regarding confidentiality.

(b) Clients have a right to confidentiality. Unless it is not feasible or is contraindicated, the discussion of confidentiality occurs at the outset of the relationship and thereafter as new circumstances may warrant.

You should discuss your client's right to confidentiality with the client and guardian at the onset of your professional relationship. If circumstances change, it is necessary to again remind the client of his or her right to confidentiality.

(c) In order to minimize intrusions on privacy, behavior analysts include only information germane to the purpose for which the communication is made in written and oral reports, consultations, and the like.

To protect your client's right to privacy, you should only include information in your verbal and written reports that is directly relevant to the behavior change under consideration.

(d) Behavior analysts discuss confidential information obtained in clinical or consulting relationships, or evaluative data concerning patients, individual or organizational clients, students, research participants, supervisees, and employees, only for appropriate scientific or professional purposes and only with persons clearly concerned with such matters.

You may share confidential information (fictitious names, location, and other identifying information should replace actual information) only with other professionals who may benefit in a scientific sense.

CASE EXAMPLE AND QUESTION 29:
DR. ELIZABETH C., JASON, AND JESSICA

Dr. Elizabeth C. was a BCBA who worked with a number of children in her small community. Dr. C. most often provided treatment in the children's homes after school hours. Two of Dr. C.'s clients, Jason and Jessica, were a brother and sister. Their alcoholic father was in and out of the home and the father had abused their mother in the past. Dr. C. attended a church where several members of the congregation knew the family. They cared very much about the children and would ask how they were doing. These caring people would often tell Dr. C. what they knew about the family and they would ask how the children were getting along in school and what kinds of things she worked on when she went to the home. The women from the church had donated clothing to the family in the past and they always had the children on the list to receive Christmas gifts from the church.

With regard to maintaining confidentiality, how much information about the children should Dr. C. give these caring church members?

MAINTAINING RECORDS (2.07)

Behavior analysts maintain appropriate confidentiality in creating, storing, accessing, transferring, and disposing of records under their control, whether these are written, automated, or in any other medium. Behavior analysts maintain and dispose of records in accordance with applicable federal or state law or regulation, and corporate policy, and in a manner that permits compliance with the requirements of these Guidelines.

You are primarily responsible for any and all records that you create, use, or store. You will need to be current with current Federal HIPAA legislation (U.S. Department of Health & Human Services, 2003).

CASE EXAMPLE AND QUESTION 30: STEVEN J.

Steven J. is a CBA who works with clients who live in a group home. He also works with the clients in the sheltered workshop they attend during the day. Steven takes data on vocational skills as well as any inappropriate behaviors occurring in the work setting. He is responsible for the behavioral component of the annual Habilitation Plan and he updates annual assessments. Steven does not have an office in his home so he has been given some file drawers in the Special Education teacher's classroom at the sheltered workshop. He keeps all of his assessment results and raw data there. The teacher locks her classroom door when she leaves for the day so that the file drawers are safe.

Does Steven's system for keeping records meet the Guidelines?

DISCLOSURES (2.08)

(a) Behavior analysts disclose confidential information without the consent of the individual only as mandated by law, or where permitted by law for a valid purpose, such as (1) to provide needed professional services to the individual or organizational client, (2) to obtain appropriate professional consultations, (3) to protect the client or others from harm, or (4) to obtain payment for services, in which instance disclosure is limited to the minimum that is necessary to achieve the purpose.

Unless your client has signed a consent form, you should not release any information about the client unless required by law. Certain circumstances may require you to release information to provide needed services for the person, to make a referral, or to collect for services rendered.

(b) Behavior analysts also may disclose confidential information with the appropriate consent of the individual or organizational client (or of another legally authorized person on behalf of the client), unless prohibited by law.

If you have written consent from your client, you may disclose confidential information.

CASE EXAMPLE AND QUESTION 31:
DR. CONNIE G. AND BILLY

Dr. Connie G. was working in a school system's prekindergarten classrooms for developmentally-disabled children. Billy was a four-year-old whose parents were divorced. Billy spent alternating weeks with each of his parents. The teacher had a theory that Billy's maladaptive behaviors, including tantrums and disruption, greatly increased on the first few days after a visit at his mother's house, so Dr. G. began taking data to evaluate this somewhat controversial notion. She felt that this sort of evaluation was simply part of her job description and did not inform the parents. At the end of the month, she submitted her time sheet indicating three hours for an evaluation of "parent-induced behavior disorder."

Is this a violation of the Guidelines?

TREATMENT EFFICACY (2.09)

(a) The behavior analyst always has the responsibility to recommend scientifically supported most effective treatment procedures. Effective treatment

procedures have been validated as having both long-term and short-term benefits to clients and society.

You should always recommend evidence-based treatments that have been shown scientifically to be effective on the short term and long term.

(b) Clients have a right to effective treatment (i.e., based on the research literature and adapted to the individual client).

It is an article of faith of behavior analysis that our clients have a right to effective treatment that has been so demonstrated in the research literature. It is the job of the behavior analyst to adapt that treatment for each individual client and then to make sure it is effective for him or her.

(c) Behavior analysts are responsible for review and appraisal of likely effects of all alternative treatments, including those provided by other disciplines and no intervention.

If your client is receiving "alternative" treatment, you are responsible for determining if there is research to support it. This may include behaviorally based treatments for which there is no evidence as well as nonbehavioral treatments that are not supported in any scientific literature. You should also be prepared to evaluate the effects of no intervention being provided.

CASE EXAMPLE AND QUESTION 32:
ROBERT AND KEVIN

Kevin is a six-year-old with DD who continues to bang his head. Robert is a CBA who has been recently assigned to Kevin's classroom. Robert's functional analysis of Kevin's behavior shows that it is related to attention from his parents and teachers. An occupational therapist (OT) has developed the current treat-

ment plan which includes sensory integration training, joint compression, and sessions three times a week to jump on a trampoline to "use up this pent up energy." The speech therapist recommended sign language. The physical therapist recommended a helmet. Kevin continued to bang his head with the helmet and he also started biting his fingers. The OT is very sure that her plan will eventually work and she explains at every treatment team meeting that everyone needs to be patient and give the sensory integration program time to work. The Special Education teacher has been, and continues to be, supportive of the OT's program.

Robert, the CBA, is clearly outnumbered here. How should he proceed?

DOCUMENTING OF PROFESSIONAL AND SCIENTIFIC WORK (2.10)

(a) Behavior analysts appropriately document their professional and scientific work in order to facilitate provision of services later by them or by other professionals, to ensure accountability, and to meet other requirements of institutions or the law.

You must maintain written records of your work product so that at some later time, other professionals may use the documentation to assist your client and to assure accountability. Keep your raw data sheets, spreadsheets, and written summaries and reports in a secure location as required by law.

(b) When behavior analysts have reason to believe that records of their professional services will be used in legal proceedings involving recipients of or participants in their work, they have a responsibility to create and maintain documentation in the kind of detail and quality that would be consistent with reasonable scrutiny in an adjudicative forum.

If there is some chance that information regarding your professional behavioral services will become part of a court case, you have an obligation to make sure that the records are complete.

CASE EXAMPLE AND QUESTION 33: DR. SANDRA M.

Dr. Sandra M. is a BCBA who is providing behavioral services to a school system that has limited services for children with autism. Dr. M. has been hired to do a very limited number of consulting hours with several children who are autistic. Dr. M. keeps the standard data expected of a behavior analyst, including baseline and treatment data. A teacher's aide collects the data twice a week. It is beginning to look like a lawsuit will be filed against the school district on behalf of its autistic students.

Considering this, what kind of records should Dr. M. be keeping to ensure the she is accountable if subpoenaed?

RECORDS AND DATA (2.11)

Behavior analysts create, maintain, disseminate, store, retain, and dispose of records and data relating to their research, practice, and other work in accordance with applicable federal and state laws or regulations and corporate policy and in a manner that permits compliance with the requirements of these Guidelines.

You will need to keep your records relating to your research and practice. This may range from ninety days to twelve years, depending on the type of records and specific regulations for state and federal laws. You will need to be in compliance with these Guidelines and check with your agency or university for specific requirements in your area.

CASE EXAMPLE AND QUESTION 34: BARBARA

In a consulting firm that hires behavior analysts, CBAs are responsible for storing their own records and data. Barbara is a CBA who is a graduate student on a limited budget. She has a typical student's apartment—small, cramped, not much storage space— and she shares it with three roommates. Barbara keeps the data for her clients for about three months and then she throws them away, but only after attending a monthly meeting where she turns in copies of her data to her supervisor.

Barbara certainly seems justified in her handling of records given her living conditions. So, is she living within the Guidelines?

FEES AND FINANCIAL ARRANGEMENTS (2.12)

(a) As early as is feasible in a professional or scientific relationship, the behavior analyst and the client or other appropriate recipient of behavior analytic services reach an agreement specifying the compensation and the billing arrangements.

As soon as you establish a professional relationship with a client (i.e., the client or his or her representative has asked you to take the case), you should inform the client (or agency) of your fees and payment policy. Although this may make you uncomfortable, it is necessary for everyone involved to avoid embarrassment, and possibly worse, later.

CASE EXAMPLE AND QUESTION 35: GLENDA

Glenda was a fourth-year graduate student in a prestigious doctoral program in behavior analysis. When she got a call from the associate chairperson of the department about an unusual case, she

jumped at the chance to get the experience and make some extra
money. She was so excited about meeting the family and the child
who was referred, she neglected to bring up her fee expectation—she
was thinking along the lines of $75 per hour because she was nearly
"a doctor" and this case did require some special expertise.

At the end of the month, when Glenda asked the associate
chairperson where she should send her bill, she was shocked and
stunned to learn that this was considered a charity case.

(b) Behavior analysts' fee practices are consistent with law and behavior
analysts do not misrepresent their fees. If limitations to services can be an-
ticipated because of limitations in financing, this is discussed with the pa-
tient, client, or other appropriate recipient of services as early as is feasible.

If state or federal law sets your fees, obey the law and clearly present your fee schedule to your client. If the client has limited funding
and this will limit behavioral services, the issue should be discussed as
soon as possible to avoid any confusion or charge of misrepresentation. Keep in mind that for a child in a school system, the "client" may
be the school system.

CASE EXAMPLE AND QUESTION 36:
JEAN A. AND WAYNE

Wayne is an eight-year-old who has moved into a new school
system in the last few weeks of the school year. He was diagnosed
as SED (severely emotionally disturbed) and he has shown some
serious behavior problems in his new classroom. Wayne will be
enrolled in the district's summer school program and Jean A., a
CBA, has been asked to work with him. The principal and
teacher met with Jean and explained to her that funding for be-
havioral services during summer school is very limited, but con-
sidering the severity of Wayne's problems, they hoped that Jean

would agree to take the case and do whatever she needs to do to meet Wayne's needs. It is clear to Jean, after some initial observations, that the funding is not adequate to provide the level of service Wayne needs.

How should Jean handle her consulting fees and the financial arrangements for this case?

ACCURACY IN REPORTS TO THOSE WHO PAY FOR SERVICES (2.13)

In their reports to those who pay for services or sources of research, project, or program funding, behavior analysts accurately state the nature of the research or service provided, the fees or charges, and where applicable, the identity of the provider, the findings, and other required descriptive data.

When handling billing information, always honestly and accurately present the necessary details regarding work completed, hours of service, and any other necessary data.

CASE EXAMPLE AND QUESTION 37

The A+ Behavior Consulting Group has a contract to provide behavioral services for five ICF/MR group homes owned by the same company. A+ has several consultants who provide the services to the group homes. Depending on scheduling, any one of several consultants may come to sit in on Habilitation Plan meetings, do assessments, and so forth. When the billing is submitted to the company owning the group homes, the name of the consultant is on the bill, the date service was provided, and the number of hours the consultant was at the facility.

Is there any other information that should be provided with the billing?

REFERRALS AND FEES (2.14)

When a behavior analyst pays, receives payment from, or divides fees with another professional other than in an employer–employee relationship, the referral shall be disclosed to the client.

Do not make it a practice to accept any form of payment for a referral. Those who do so put their reputation at risk and must disclose this information immediately to the client.

CASE EXAMPLE AND QUESTION 38: BARRY

A large consulting firm of clinical psychologists has several psychologists on staff who specialize in psychological testing. Barry S., a CBA, knows some of the psychologists through work he has done in the schools. One of the clinical psychologists in this group has approached Barry and told him that the firm would pay him a $25 referral fee for each client he referred to the group for testing. Barry is an ethical CBA who would only refer clients who needed a psychological work-up.

Because he knows these psychologists and respects their diagnostic skills, under what conditions would this arrangement be acceptable?

INTERRUPTING OR TERMINATING SERVICES (2.15)

(a) Behavior analysts make reasonable efforts to plan for facilitating care in the event that behavior analytic services are interrupted by factors such as the behavior analyst's illness, impending death, unavailability, or relocation or by the client's relocation or financial limitations.

For each of your clients, you should have a plan to provide coverage in the event that you are no longer able to do so. Interruption of service applies to temporarily stopping services by the behavior analyst, often due to the behavior analyst's health or family problems. Interrupting services does not mean canceling sessions for a short time, as when the behavior analyst has the flu or takes a vacation. The interruption of services refers to stopping services for an extended period of time, such as a month or longer.

(b) When entering into employment or contractual relationships, behavior analysts provide for orderly and appropriate resolution of responsibility for client care in the event that the employment or contractual relationship ends, with paramount consideration given to the welfare of the client.

If you are working through an agency that has a contract with clients for services, read the contract carefully so you understand what will happen to the clients if you are unable to provide consulting for an extended period of time. The welfare of each client should be of utmost importance to you should this occur.

CASE EXAMPLE AND QUESTION 39: DR. MARTHA D.

Dr. Martha D. has been providing behavioral services to the six young women who live in a group home. Dr. D. has developed a health problem requiring surgery and a lengthy recovery period. Dr. D. is attached to these young women and does not want to give up this contract, but her surgery and follow-up recovery is not optional. She would like to resume her consulting when she is better. Her best estimate is that she would be away from the group home for about three months.

Because she will be gone so long, does Dr. D. need to resign from this job in the best interest of the clients?

(c) Behavior analysts do not abandon clients. Behavior analysts terminate a professional relationship when it becomes reasonably clear that the client no longer needs the service, is not benefiting, or is being harmed by continued service.

Do not walk away from your clients without notice. You may terminate a professional relationship when (a) it is clear that the client no longer needs your service, (b) you determine that the client is not benefiting, or (c) you establish that the client is actually being harmed in some way by your service.

(d) Prior to termination for whatever reason, except where precluded by the client's conduct, the behavior analyst discusses the client's views and needs, provides appropriate pre-termination services, suggests alternative service providers as appropriate, and takes other reasonable steps to facilitate transfer of responsibility to another provider if the client needs one immediately.

If you need to terminate your service, you should discuss the client's needs with the relevant parties (e.g., parents, guardian, agency director, school administrator) and suggest other professionals who can provide assistance.

CASE EXAMPLE AND QUESTION 40: MARCUS

Marcus is a ten-year-old who was physically and verbally abused while living with his biological mother. Protective Services removed him from the home and he now lives with his biological father. A CBA has been assigned to work in the home several hours per week. Marcus has been prescribed medication for hyperactivity, but his dad does not give it to him on a consistent basis. The dad has refused parent training, and further says he does not need anyone telling him how to handle his child's behavior. When the CBA comes to the home, the dad uses the visit as a chance to have a free babysitter.

It feels like it is impossible to get any cooperation with behavioral services in this home, but can the CBA justify leaving this child?

RESPONSES TO CASE QUESTION 25: TERRY

The CBAs responsibility is to all parties affected by behavioral services. The CBA has a responsibility to family members to involve them from the beginning, especially because the behavior also occurs at home. If the parents were unable to come to the school, they should have been notified immediately, by the CBA, via a phone call.

RESPONSES TO CASE QUESTION 26: DR. ROBERT M. AND JERRY

No, Dr. M. is a BCBA and although he may be widely read, he is not trained as a sex therapist or counselor. Teaching Jerry "to verbalize about sex-related issues" does not make this a behavioral problem. With appropriate consent from Jerry and his parents, Dr. M. should refer Jerry to a properly trained and certified counselor who can help him sort through his problems.

RESPONSES TO CASE QUESTION 27: DR. B.

On his arrival at the facility, Dr. B. should have a meeting with the administrator to clarify his relationship with the Developmental Disability Department and his role at the facility. He should set up some routine reporting procedures such as weekly meetings with key administrators, including brief written reports of his findings. He has taken this position because he believes he can help the facility, but everyone needs to be aware of who he is actually working for and attempts to influence his judgment need to be turned away.

RESPONSES TO CASE QUESTION 28: SUSAN P. AND SARA

The behavior analyst must support the rights of clients. At any time a client is recorded (audio or video), consent must be granted. Further, if you get permission to tape a session for one purpose and then decide to do something additional with the tape, you must again obtain permission. At the beginning of working with any client (and his or her family or guardian, in the case of a minor), the CBA should inform that client of procedures to complain about the professional practices of the behavior analyst. Susan, although not a CBA, clearly violated the spirit of these Guidelines and should apologize to the mother and report to her major professor about this incident.

RESPONSES TO CASE QUESTION 29: DR. ELIZABETH C., JASON, AND JESSICA

Behavior analysts have an obligation to respect the confidentiality of those with whom they work. When asked about the children, Dr. C. should politely tell anyone who asks that she cannot discuss her work with her clients. She should then politely change the subject.

RESPONSES TO CASE QUESTION 30: STEVEN J.

Although keeping records in the office of another professional is a frequent practice, this should not be done unless the CBA has file drawers to which he has the only keys. Although the teacher locks her classroom door at the end of the day, when Steven is not at the facility, the teacher, her aide, or anyone with access to the classroom could view the confidential information in the records.

RESPONSES TO CASE QUESTION 31: DR. CONNIE G. AND BILLY

Although 2.06 addresses confidentiality, 2.08 gives the behavior analyst the right to disclose information without the consent of the client to obtain payment for services. A key distinction here is that disclosure is limited to the minimum necessary information to achieve the purpose. This means that Dr. C. should not include confidential information in her report other than the minimum amount of information required for billing.

RESPONSES TO CASE QUESTION 32: ROBERT AND KEVIN

Robert should explain to the team that clients have a right to effective treatment. His professional responsibility is to review and evaluate alternative treatments and he should request empirically-based articles from these other professionals and critique them. A baseline should be started as soon as possible. Emergency procedures should be used if Kevin is hurting himself. Interventions for SIB should be based on the research literature, and if Robert is not satisfied that these "other" treatments are supported by empirical evidence, he should say so at the next habilitation team meeting.

RESPONSES TO CASE QUESTION 33: DR. SANDRA M.

The Guidelines say that work should be documented to ensure accountability and to meet other requirements. Therefore, at a minimum, Dr. M. would want to have data as described in 3.0 (Assessment) and 4.0 (Behavior Change Programs) of the Guidelines. Further, Dr. M. should be sure that she has collected some sample of the data herself. In addition to data, detailed case notes would be helpful. If there are any observations related to students being affected by a lack of services or resources, this should be noted with relevant specifics.

RESPONSES TO CASE QUESTION 34: BARBARA

Barbara is keeping records in her apartment. Can the roommates see the records? The records should be locked so that she has the only access. Throwing client records in the trash is not a good idea. Sometimes trash cans are turned over, sanitation department workers drop things when emptying cans into the truck, and so forth. Client records that are thrown away should be shredded. Three months is not long enough to keep records. Barbara should be complying with state laws and other relevant (e.g., Medicaid) requirements. In most states, records should be kept for at least three years. Finally, if a consulting firm hires Barbara, this firm should have an office or storage location where records can be maintained appro-

priately. This is especially important for companies that retain the services of graduate students who are likely to graduate and move away.

RESPONSES TO CASE QUESTION 35: GLENDA

Had Glenda inquired about her payment for taking this case on the front end she might not have gotten it. It was valuable experience and it did enhance the departments' image as a caring organization which can help out those in need in a pinch. And, it was a valuable lesson for Glenda that she would not soon forget as she prepared to take comps and move into the real world.

RESPONSES TO CASE QUESTION 36: JEAN A. AND WAYNE

Jean and the principal can quickly make an appeal to the district and other support services for getting additional hours approved for behavioral services. If this doesn't work, Jean needs to estimate the number of hours she can work given the funding in the budget. She needs to discuss and put in writing the limitations to services. As a last resort, Jean can start training a school staff person to assist with the services she is providing. She may be able to be on-site less if someone else who has the appropriate skill level can assist with Wayne's behavioral program.

RESPONSES TO CASE QUESTION 37

The billing should also include the specific nature of the service provided, the findings, and any recommendations.

RESPONSES TO CASE QUESTION 38: BARRY

The Guidelines state that referral fees can be accepted, but they must be disclosed with the client or agency. In this case, to remain within the Guidelines, Barry would have to tell the school that he was suggesting that this firm do the testing and that he would receive referral fees. Depending on how this was handled and how often it happened, this situation could border on a conflict of interest. The safest bet for the ethical behavior analyst is to never accept referral fees.

RESPONSES TO CASE QUESTION 39: DR. MARTHA D.

It is acceptable for behavior analysts to interrupt their services as long as they provide for the orderly and systematic care of the clients. Dr. D. needs to talk with the agency as soon as possible, tell the appropriate personnel she would like to continue, and give the timelines expected for her recovery. Dr. D. can suggest someone to cover for her while she is out on leave and she can develop a plan for that person to use while she is gone. When she is feeling better, she can check in by phone.

RESPONSES TO CASE QUESTION 40: MARCUS

This is clearly a very sad situation for Marcus. However, it is reasonably clear that given the current situation, Marcus is not benefiting from the behavioral services at this time. The CBA needs to terminate this relationship. She should document everything she has tried to do and the noncompliance on the dad's part. The documentation should be provided to Protective Services as well as the other relevant agencies.

Chapter 6

Assessing Behavior (Guideline 3)

It is a bedrock principle of behavior analysis that it is necessary to "take a baseline" before any treatment is contemplated. The reasons are not so obvious to outsiders and the methodology by which it is accomplished is out of the reach of most other professions. For us, taking a baseline means many things, including the following: a referral has been made of a behavior that is problematic; the behavior is observable and has been operationally defined in some manner that allows quantification; and, on several occasions, a trained observer has visited the setting where the behavior occurs and has documented the occurrence and the circumstances under which it occurs (this indicates that the referral is legitimate, that the problem is measurable, and that the behavior may or may not require treatment, depending on what the graphs of the data show). Behavior analysts don't work on rumor or hearsay. They want to see the problem for themselves, to get some sense of the variability from day to day, to determine if there is any trending, and finally, they want to understand the circumstances under which the behavior occurs and to get some sense of the function of the behavior.

"This kid is driving me crazy, he is constantly out of his seat, talking with the other children, and he never completes an assignment that I hand out. I spend all my time sending him back to his seat and telling him to sit down." This referral from a very frustrated third-grade teacher would be the stimulus for a behavior analyst to go to the classroom and observe exactly what is going on. (The teacher, meanwhile, was thinking that she would like to get this "brat" out of her classroom.) Although the assistant principal, school counselor, or school psychologist might immediately start giving the teacher some advice on what to do or schedule a battery of IQ and personality tests, the behavior analyst insists that some assessment of the behavior occur first. How much time is the boy out of his seat? What was the stimulus for this behavior? What kind of assignments are given and how many does he actually complete? The behavior analyst will also be interested in knowing what kind of prompts the teacher uses for each of the behaviors and what type of reinforcement she currently uses to maintain the behavior (if any). Another question that might come up has to do with the appropriateness of the class assignments for the student. Is there any chance that they are too difficult or that the instructions are inadequate? And finally, the behavior analyst, while observing the referred student, will also be assessing the degree of peer involvement in this child's behavior. The astute and ethical behavior analyst will take enough baseline to assure that there is indeed a problem that needs solving and will have some preliminary ideas as to the variables that might be operating. One final point is that this baseline data will be graphed and used in an evaluation of treatment effects. Imagine how this would work if there was no rule about taking a baseline first. The behavior analyst would have to rely on an untrained, possibly biased person's estimate of the frequency of the target behaviors, would have to take this person's opinion of likely causal variables seriously, and have no basis for evaluation of any suggestions made. Viewed in this light, it's downright unethical to operate in this fashion, and yet this scenario is probably the mode for what passes as behavior consulting in America by nonbehavioral "professionals."

The BACB® Guidelines clearly specify what goes into a behavioral assessment and further includes an even broader obligation to explain to the client (which may include the teacher, principal, and parents) the conditions necessary for the intervention to work (3.08) and those that might prevent it from being properly implemented (3.01, 3.02). If the ethical behavior analyst determines what the controlling variables are through a functional assessment (see Iwata, Dorsey, Slifer, Bauman, &

Richman, 1982, for the original study on this method), she is obligated to spell this out for the clients and to explain the limiting conditions for treatment. This latter concept, limiting conditions, is critical to an understanding of how behavior analysis works in applied settings. To take a simple example, if we want to use a reinforcer to strengthen the sitting-in-seat behavior of the third grader described earlier, we have to find out what is the reinforcer. If, for some reason, we are not able to find a reinforcer, then this limiting condition has been exceeded. Or, if we discover what the reinforcer is but are not allowed to use it, or if the teacher refuses to use the reinforcer even if we know what it is, we have exceeded one of the limiting conditions of treatment. If the reinforcer is some sort of snack (discovered through a reinforcer assessment) but the teacher "doesn't believe in using snacks," then it will be difficult to change this child's behavior through this means. Or, if the behavior analyst determines that a daily report card is the best solution for the child but the parents refuse to cooperate by delivering contingent reinforcers at home, we have run headlong into a limiting condition of treatment.

A final note on assessment: It is so important that behavior analysts explain to the client what the data means (probably using actual working graphs to illustrate the key points), that we have determined that it should be included in the Guidelines. There, in Guideline 3.09, it is clearly stated that as a behavior analyst, you have an obligation to explain the baseline data, functional assessment, reinforcement assessment, or other forms of behavioral data collection to the client, in plain English, so he or she can understand what is involved. This includes, of course, the results of any interventions to show actual measured effects of what was tried and what worked. Besides keeping the client, guardian, or advocate apprised of our interventions, this requirement also probably serves some public relations function. It teaches the client that what we do is transparent and understandable, that we are objective in our approach, and that we use data for decision making. One hoped-for result is that clients and client-surrogates so educated will begin to ask questions of other professionals about the basis for their interventions.

ASSESSING BEHAVIOR (3.0)

Behavior analysts who use behavioral assessment techniques do so for purposes that are appropriate in light of the research.

This statement refers to those behavior analysts who perhaps use more standardized behavioral assessments than simply taking a baseline. The thrust of this recommendation is that the behavior analyst is obligated to learn about the research associated with the assessment and to make sure that it is used within the boundaries of reliability and validity that have been established for the assessment.

(a) Behavior analysts' assessments, recommendations, reports, and evaluative statements are based on information and techniques sufficient to provide appropriate substantiation for their findings.

Behavior analysts present their findings based on assessment tools that are up to the task scientifically. This means knowing precisely how the standardization sample compares with the client being evaluated and being able to interpret the results using the test manual and associated research that may have been done with the assessment.

(b) Behavior analysts refrain from misuse of assessment techniques, interventions, results, and interpretations and take reasonable steps to prevent others from misusing the information these techniques provide.

The most likely form of misuse of an assessment is to go beyond the data that is actually collected. We do not overstate the results of our assessment results and discourage others from doing so.

(c) Behavior analysts recognize limits to the certainty with which judgments or predictions can be made about individuals.

As behavioral scientists, we stay very close to the data rather than make unsubstantiated predictions about behavior. We frequently use qualifiers such as "my best judgment is" or "it seems to me that ...," and we usually acknowledge that our assessment is not perfect or definitive, for example, we might say, "Based on three days of observation, I would say that Carl's behavior is more likely to occur when he is asked to do math problems," rather than "Carl is math phobic." In cases where nonbehavioral assessments are provided to a behavior analyst, the behavior analyst conducts behavior assessments (i.e., functional analysis, data collection, direct observation of behaviors) before planning a behavior program.

CASE EXAMPLE AND QUESTION 41A:
THERESA H. AND CHARLIE

Theresa H., a CBA who was providing behavioral consultation for adults who were profoundly mentally retarded, was provided with assessment materials for Charlie, a new client at a residential facility. Charlie's folder included the results from Stanford Binet and Wechsler IQ tests. Charlie was a verbal client and he appeared to have good self-help and social skills. However, because his IQ test scores were listed as "untestable," the facility administrator felt that Charlie should start in basic training classes at the facility rather than in the sheltered workshop setting. The administrator said if Charlie "proved himself," he could transition to sheltered work in a few months.

Theresa felt very uneasy about the test results, but she was not sure if she should question the work of another professional and the administrator. What do you think?

(d) Behavior analysts do not promote the use of behavioral assessment techniques by unqualified persons, i.e., those who are unsupervised by experienced professionals and have not demonstrated valid and reliable assessment skills.

Behavior analysts are very particular about data collection and insist that only those who are well trained should be involved in this aspect of assessment. Work that is done by CABA should be supervised by a CBA or BCBA.

CASE EXAMPLE AND QUESTION 41B:

THERESA H. AND CHARLIE

In the aforementioned scenario, after calling the previous facility, Theresa received some assessment information that was behavior analytic in nature. She was relieved to see a functional analysis. The functional analysis and other behavioral assessments were done by a CABA. Theresa called the facility again to ask if there was any additional assessment information or data and to get the name of the CBA who supervised the CABA. It seems that the facility did not have a CBA and the CABA was doing the best she knew how to provide behavioral assessments and treatment for clients.

In light of this information, how should Theresa proceed. Is she ready to start an intervention?

ENVIRONMENTAL CONDITIONS THAT PRECLUDE IMPLEMENTATION (3.01)

If environmental conditions preclude implementation of a behavior analytic program, the behavior analyst recommends that other professional assistance (i.e., assessment, consultation, or therapeutic intervention by other professionals) be sought.

In most circumstances a behavior analyst, having conducted a behavioral assessment, is going to recommend some sort of behavioral treatment. However, if no CABA or CBA is available to implement the treatment, or if there are no resources available to fund a behavioral treatment, the behavior analyst will refer the case to another professional.

CASE EXAMPLE AND QUESTION 42: DAVID K.

David K. is a CBA who was recently asked to provide services to a program for adults with developmental disabilities. David went to visit the program and was dismayed to see a building that was a mess, a lack of materials for training, a number of clients with behavior problems, and a very serious shortage of staff. David asked about the staffing at the facility and was told that due to budget cuts, almost every day there was not enough staff. With regard to implementing behavior programs, this situation was in the no-win category. David felt sorry for the clients and wanted to help. He was considering accepting the position and doing as much as he could by filling in as an extra pair of hands until additional staff could be hired.

If you were David, what would you do?

ENVIRONMENTAL CONDITIONS THAT HAMPER IMPLEMENTATION (3.02)

If environmental conditions hamper implementation of the behavior analytic program, the behavior analyst seeks to eliminate the environmental constraints, or identifies in writing the obstacles to doing so.

Behavior programs require certain minimum conditions (e.g., a stable environment, some control over reinforcers, consistency in the delivery of consequences) to be effective. The behavior analyst will identify these "environmental constraints" and attempt to modify or eliminate them prior to implementing a behavior program. If this is not possible, then the behavior analyst will put in writing a description of these conditions.

CASE EXAMPLE AND QUESTION 43:
DR. PATTI S.

Dr. Patti S., a BCBA, was providing behavioral services to a large inner city preschool program for children with disabilities. The program did a good job with regard to providing the support necessary for behavioral programming to be effective. However, a new early childhood administrator came to the district and decided that prekindergarten staff would be intensively trained off-site in the High Scope (developmental) curriculum model. This newly-required intensive training for staff resulted in classes being short-staffed nearly every day. The staff who remained at the facility were scrambling to meet the basic needs of the children; they no longer had time to take data, implement interventions, and so forth.

What is Dr. S.'s first step in handling this situation?

FUNCTIONAL ASSESSMENT (3.03)

(a) The behavior analyst conducts a functional assessment, as defined below, to provide the necessary data to develop an effective behavior change program.

It is now considered "best practice" for behavior analysis to determine the function of a behavior prior to writing a behavior program.

CASE EXAMPLE AND QUESTION 44:
CASSANDRA P. AND DEBBIE

Cassandra P. was a CBA who was called to a facility to address the behavior problems of Debbie, a twenty-four-year-old woman who was severely retarded. Debbie would sit at the window and scream and then she would pull out handfuls of her own hair. The direct care staff and facility behavior specialist wanted Cassandra to start an intervention immediately. They all told Cassandra they had observed this behavior over several weeks, there was no apparent cause, and this was a behavior that occurred for no reason "out of the blue."

Because the behavior is self-injurious, should Cassandra begin an intervention immediately?

(b) Functional assessment includes a variety of systematic information-gathering activities regarding factors influencing the occurrence of a behavior (e.g., antecedents, consequences, setting events, or establishing operations) including interview, direct observation, and experimental analysis.

Functional assessment may range from an informal descriptive analysis (based on interviews and informal observations), to a more formal data-based observation system, to an actual experimental functional assessment as is often seen in the *Journal of Applied Behavior Analysis (JABA)*. The goal of a functional assessment is to determine what the controlling variables are for the behavior in question. Sometimes this is obvious just from watching the individual for a few sessions; in other cases, it is necessary to interview staff members or teachers to get some inkling of what motivates the behavior. Finally, in some cases, the controlling variables are so subtle that it takes an experimental protocol to discover an effective independent variable.

CASE EXAMPLE AND QUESTION 45:
FLORENCE AND SONDRA

Florence worked as a supervisor in a residential facility for multiply handicapped individuals. One of her residents, Sondra, had a strange behavior that involved pulling at her hair at various times during the day. She had clear bald spots and her scalp was often red and tender. Using what she learned about functional analysis from workshops at a state convention of behavior analysts, Florence started some informal observations. She concluded that Sondra's hair-pulling was more likely to occur right before meals and was perhaps a "frustration response" to not being able to eat when she wanted. Florence arranged for Sondra to have nutritious snacks while the meal was being prepared and for her to eat first to eliminate the frustration. After a month, it appeared that Sondra's hair-pulling was unaffected. Next, Florence called in her BCBA and asked for help. She showed the CBA her data and told him about the informal functional assessment. The CBA then began time-sampling several times per day to produce a more precise descriptive analysis. The CBA's data showed that although some of the hair-pulling occurred before meals, even more was occurring after Sondra went to bed. He felt that the source of the agitation was a roommate whose television was too loud. The CBA arranged for a test of this hypothesis by switching Sondra's roommate on four separate nights over the next month. In no case was the hair-pulling observed.

Is an experimental functional analysis necessary in this case?

ACCEPTING CLIENTS (3.04)

The behavior analyst accepts as clients only those individuals or entities (agencies, firms, etc.) whose behavior problems or requested service are commensurate with the behavior analyst's education, training, and experience. In lieu of these conditions, the behavior analyst must function under the supervision of or in consultation with a behavior analyst whose credentials permit working with such behavior problems or services.

Behavior analysts understand and acknowledge the limitations of their expertise. If they are working on cases beyond their range of experience and training, behavior analysts will seek supervision from someone with proper credentials to assure that they are operating ethically and to avoid doing any harm.

CASE EXAMPLE AND QUESTION 46:
MARTIN K. AND DAN

Martin K. was CBA who moved to a new city to work at a large state hospital for persons with mental health problems. This was a new area of expertise for Martin; his past experience was limited to clients who were profoundly retarded with multiple physical disabilities. At the new state hospital setting, one of the clients Martin was assigned to was Dan, a twenty-three-year-old man who had a severe head injury. As a result of his head injury, Dan engaged in violent and dangerous outbursts of aggression. Dan's aggressive outbursts had resulted in more than one staff person needing medical treatment. Martin was eager to help Dan and he began reading everything he could about head injury. Martin felt that the state hospital hired him to do a job and assigned him to this client and he was committed to getting Dan's behavior under control.

Apart from reading all he can to learn about head injury, is there anything else that Martin should be doing?

CONSENT—CLIENT RECORDS (3.05)

The behavior analyst obtains the written consent of the client or client-surrogate before obtaining or disclosing client records from or to other sources.

It is occasionally necessary for a behavior analyst to share information about a case with another professional or an agency. In those cases, the behavior analyst obtains written permission from the client to do so.

CASE EXAMPLE AND QUESTION 47:
DR. STUART W. AND TOM

Dr. Stuart W., a BCBA, has been working on Tom's behavioral issues for two years. Tom lives in a supported living apartment in the community and he works at a job with supervision from Vocational Rehabilitation. Dr. W.'s data shows that Tom frequently arrives late or completely misses work. Tom would rather stay home and sleep and a variety of incentive programs has been ineffective. Dr. W. is wondering if Tom would benefit from counseling. He has a friend and colleague who is a counselor. Dr. W.'s plan to is to invite his colleague to lunch and tell him about Tom.

Can Dr. W. ethically talk to another professional about Tom to determine if the person would consider taking Tom as a client?

DESCRIBING PROGRAM OBJECTIVES (3.06)

(a) The behavior analyst describes, preferably in writing, the objectives of the behavior change program to the client or client-surrogate (see below) before attempting to implement the program.

It is considered standard practice for behavior analysts to specify in writing the objectives of all behavior programs. This statement of objectives should be shared with the client or the client's representative.

(b) As used here, client-surrogate refers to someone legally empowered to make decisions for the person(s) whose behavior the program is intended to change; examples of client-surrogates include parents of minors, guardians, legally designated representatives.

"Client-surrogate" means a person who has been legally designated to represent the client's interests.

CASE EXAMPLE AND QUESTION 48A:
ANGIE AND SUSAN

Susan is a fifty-two-year-old woman with developmental disabilities. She lives at home with her mother who is her legal guardian and she attends a vocational training program. Susan is a client of developmental services and she receives behavioral programming as needed. Angie is a CBA who works with clients at the vocational program. Angie has been asked to provide behavioral services for Susan. It seems that Susan has been spending all of her money on junk food. Then, so that she has money, she has been asking staff to give her loans or pay her for small favors. This behavior has escalated to the point that Susan has no money for bus transportation and she is making everyone uncomfortable with her begging. Because begging is not really an appropriate behavior, Angie feels that it would be okay to instruct the staff to immediately begin treating begging with social disapproval.

At what point does Angie need to get approval from Susan's mother?

BEHAVIORAL ASSESSMENT APPROVAL (3.07)

The behavior analyst must obtain the client's or client-surrogate's approval in writing of the behavior assessment procedures before implementing them.

Before any baseline or functional assessment procedures are begun, the behavior analyst must have the approval of the client or the client's representative.

CASE EXAMPLE AND QUESTION 48B:
ANGIE AND SUSAN

Susan, the client in the aforementioned scenario, is about to begin her behavior program for spending all of her money and begging. The CBA, Angie, did contact Susan's mother and tell her about the objectives of the behavior plan.

Is there anything else that Angie needs to discuss with Susan's mom?

DESCRIBING CONDITIONS FOR PROGRAM SUCCESS (3.08)

The behavior analyst describes to the client or client-surrogate the environmental conditions that are necessary for the program to be effective.

Prior to the implementation of a program, the behavior analyst describes to the client or the client's representative, the conditions believed necessary for the program to work effectively. This can actually be a rather complex matter because it has to be stated as a series of contingency statements. It is almost always necessary to find the function of the behavior, then to find some way to gain control over the key maintaining variables. If this includes reinforcement, some way of making it contingent on appropriate behavior has to be arranged, on a consistent basis without causing satiation. And, the program has to be designed in such a way that the client does not suddenly engage in escape behavior.

CASE EXAMPLE AND QUESTION 49A:
PHYLLIS AND ROSEMARY

Rosemary is a thirty-two-year-old woman who has behavior problems and moderate mental retardation. She lives in a residential facility and attends a workshop during the day. Rosemary has some unusual behaviors with regard to her dressing and appearance. She is nearly 100 pounds overweight, is buxom, and she refuses to wear a bra. She wears skirts that she rolls up at the waistband to make the skirts extremely short. If staff do not intervene, Rosemary tries to leave the facility in the morning wearing an excessive amount of makeup. These behaviors have been documented by Phyllis, the CBA. Phyllis has been asked to design an intervention. Rosemary would no doubt be embarrassed if someone told her the behaviors were a problem and an intervention would be started soon.

How would you handle the situation with regard to Rosemary?

EXPLAINING ASSESSMENT RESULTS (3.09)

Unless the nature of the relationship is clearly explained to the person being assessed in advance and precludes provision of an explanation of results (such as in some organizational consulting, some screenings, and forensic evaluations), behavior analysts ensure that an explanation of the results is provided using language that is reasonably understandable to the person assessed or to another legally authorized person on behalf of the client. Regardless of whether the interpretation is done by the behavior analyst, by as-

sistants, others, behavior analysts take reasonable steps to ensure that appropriate explanations of results are given.

Behavior analysts explain the results of the assessment, in plain English, to the client or the client's representative. There may be some exceptions, but this is the general rule because in behavior analysis we seek transparency with all our methods.

CASE EXAMPLE AND QUESTION 49B: ROSEMARY

In the aforementioned case with Rosemary, if we found that her behavior was a function of lack of stimulating materials in the workshop, that the workshop staff failed to provide any reinforcement for on-task or task completion, that Rosemary was not paid for the work she did, and finally that her dressing style appeared to be maintained by her boyfriend who she would meet at a motel not far from the workshop, what would you do by way of explaining these results to her?

RESPONSES TO CASE QUESTION 41A: THERESA H. AND CHARLIE

IQ tests are not a good behavioral measure of a person's ability. They are particularly not the best method of measuring the abilities of a person with profound mental retardation. Theresa needs to have Charlie quickly evaluated using an assessment tool that measures adaptive behaviors and functional skills. Theresa can tell the administrator that behavior analysts are bound by the Guidelines to provide appropriate assessments.

RESPONSES TO CASE QUESTION 41B: THERESA H. AND CHARLIE

Theresa needs to administer the functional assessment and take the baseline data on Charlie's behavior problems again. She needs to do this in order to have an assessment in the new setting. She also needs to do this because, although the CABA was doing her best, her work should have been supervised and signed off on by a CBA.

RESPONSES TO CASE QUESTION 42: DAVID K.

We would advise David not to take the position. This critical shortage of staff will prevent the implementation of behavior programs. When the facility is adequately staffed, David can offer to provide behavioral services.

RESPONSES TO CASE QUESTION 43: DR. PATTI S.

Dr. S. needs to identify in writing for the principal and school's prekindergarten district administrator the environmental (staffing) problems that are hampering the implementation of behavioral programs.

RESPONSES TO CASE QUESTION 44:
CASSANDRA P. AND DEBBIE

When a client is engaging in self-injury, it is appropriate to put emergency procedures in place. In fact, this should always be done. However, after ensuring the client is safe (and implementing an emergency procedure, if necessary), prior to any intervention, the first step to treating this behavior is a functional assessment. Functional assessment can include informal procedures such as interviews and informal observations. When staff members say that a behavior is "out of the blue" or it occurs "all of the time," it is usually a clue that the behavior analyst should do some observing on his or her own.

RESPONSES TO CASE QUESTION 45:
FLORENCE AND SONDRA

Florence would not need to carry out an experimental functional assessment if the information she got from the informal analysis was adequate to develop an effective intervention.

RESPONSES TO CASE QUESTION 46: MARTIN K. AND DAN

Because behavior analysts should only accept clients whose behavior problems are commensurate with the behavior analyst's skill level, Martin needs to consult with a CBA who is an expert in the treatment of aggression and head injury. If there is no such person at the facility, he needs to find someone in the area to supervise him. There can be liability issues if he does not.

RESPONSES TO CASE QUESTION 47: DR. STUART W. AND TOM

Dr. W. must obtain the written consent of the client (Tom) or his guardian before disclosing Tom's records or giving information such as his name or behavioral specifics to another professional, regardless of the purpose.

RESPONSES TO CASE QUESTION 48A: ANGIE AND SUSAN

Before implementing any procedures to change Susan's behavior, Angie needs to outline the objectives of the behavior plan in writing for Susan's mother (her legal guardian). It could be that the mother feels Susan has the right to spend her money on snacks as long as she goes to work. The intervention for this problem may well be something for which the mother wishes to have some input.

RESPONSES TO CASE QUESTION 48B: ANGIE AND SUSAN

Because Susan may be getting some of her money from home and it is the money that is related to the problem, Angie needs to talk to Susan's mom about the environmental conditions that are necessary for the behavior program to be effective. For example, if we are trying to reinforce Susan for managing her money, it will not help if he mom is giving Susan extra money that we don't know about.

RESPONSES TO CASE QUESTION 49A:
PHYLLIS AND ROSEMARY

In the case of a client who is lower functioning than Rosemary, a behavior analyst would discuss the results of any behavioral assessment with the guardian or some other legally authorized person. In Rosemary's case, the assessment findings pertain to adaptive behaviors. Phyllis should definitely talk to Rosemary about her findings. Phyllis can explain to Rosemary that everyone wants Rosemary to succeed and Phyllis will be starting a plan to help her.

RESPONSES TO CASE QUESTION 49B: ROSEMARY

The Guidelines stress that no matter what the setting, behavior analysts use language that is understandable to the person assessed. In this case, Phyllis should attempt to let Rosemary know that she understands that the workshop setting is boring to her and that spending time with her boyfriend is important. It might not be possible to explain much more to her but the other details should be easy to explain to Rosemary's surrogate or guardian. A reinforcement program could be put in place to make work at the workshop more appealing (e.g., Rosemary could earn money to buy nice clothes), and an acceptable plan for seeing the boyfriend could be implemented (e.g., date night). This assumes that the boyfriend is an "approved" person in Rosemary's life, that there are two consenting adults, and he is not using Rosemary or taking advantage of her.

A female staff person could work with Rosemary to help her select an attractive wardrobe and apply makeup that is tasteful. Rosemary's behavior suggests that she is trying to make herself more appealing and she needs guidance, education, and possibly a fashion and makeup makeover.

Chapter 7

The Behavior Analyst and the Individual Behavior Change Program (Guideline 4)

As alluded to in chapter 4, in the early evolution of the field, behavior analysts had a modus operandi of carrying out behavior change programs that could be described positively by supporters as "fluid" and by detractors as "making-it-up-as-they-go-along." In the beginning, behavior programs were just extensions of laboratory procedures with adaptations for humans and the settings they occupied. Nothing was written down and there was no approval process per se. Data was always collected, usually with precision and consistency, and the results were so novel and amazing that all of those involved would marvel at the effects they were seeing with these primitive procedures. With success came recognition of the seriousness of the mission these early pioneers had undertaken. They quickly realized that these were not just experiments in behavior change but rather a totally new form of therapy, data-based to be sure, but therapy nonetheless. And therapy required a new level of care, consideration, thoughtfulness, and responsibility. It became clear that better record keeping would be required. By the mid-1980s, behavior analysis practitioners were fully in compliance with standards of the time, which required that the client, or a surrogate, actually approve the program in writing before it was implemented. This increased responsibility and accountability also meant that other protocols must be followed as well, such as using least-restrictive procedures,[1] avoiding harmful consequences (including both reinforcers and punishers), and involving the client in any modifications to programs that might be made along the way. Skinner (1953) had always been against the use of punishers, but it took the field of behavior analysis quite a while to codify some statement on this. It was the vetting of these Guidelines that finally resulted in a concise and cohesive position: "The behavior analyst recommends reinforcement rather than punishment whenever possible." The essence of this aspect of the Guidelines is to inform consumers and remind behavior analysts that, as a field, we are primarily interested in developing behavior change programs that teach new, appropriate, adaptive behaviors using nonharmful reinforcers whenever possible.

One interesting feature of Guideline 4.0 is that we make it explicit that our form of therapy involves "on-going data collection." When compared with other forms of treatment, this presents one of the most unique and valuable features. Ongoing, objective data collection helps the behavior analyst understand the effect of treatment and the consumer is able to make an ongoing evaluation of the worth of the treatment as well.

At the onset of a behavior change program, most of the focus is on finding just the right treatment and implementing it correctly, under

---

[1]The term *least restrictive* does not always make sense when applied to procedures as opposed to environments. In the original Wyatt v. Stickney (1971) case, a patient kept in an institution (clearly restrictive with locked wards and seclusion rooms) who could be treated in the community (clearly less restrictive by comparison) was entitled to be treated in "the least restrictive *environment*." When applied to treatments, "least restrictive" suggests that some procedures like time-out are probably more restrictive than DRO, for example. A physical or mechanical restraint is likewise more restrictive than time-out. Or is it? Time-out requires that the person be removed from the environment, perhaps to a place where he or she cannot see others. Is this more or less restrictive? And, what about punishment? Is a sharp "No!" contingent on behavior "restrictive?" Other aversive stimuli such as water mist or lemon juice would also be included in this category.

safe conditions. One additional requirement for behavior analysts is that some consideration be given to the termination criteria. Basically, we need to ask, "When will we stop treatment?" It is presumed that termination comes when the consumer's behavior has been sufficiently changed to warrant cessation, but what is the criterion? There is a great deal of "clinical judgment" involved in this decision, and of course, the client or his or her surrogate must also be involved. By requiring that some thought be given to what level of behavior change is desired, the Guidelines prevent open-ended treatment that goes on and on. If the behavior analyst is treating SIB, for example, he or she must indicate, and get approval for, some level of acceptable behavior change. "Zero SIB for two weeks" might be one such goal. Or, if the behavior change program involves an adaptive behavior, the goal might state, "Carl will be able to completely dress himself, without any assistance, for three consecutive days." As often happens, the client or the client's surrogate might at that point decide to terminate treatment, or, as often happens, another goal might be set such as, "Carl will be able to ride the bus independently for one week" or "Carl will be able to complete a full work day with no SIB or inappropriate behavior."

THE BEHAVIOR ANALYST AND THE INDIVIDUAL BEHAVIOR CHANGE PROGRAM (4.0)

The behavior analyst designs programs that are based on behavior analytic principles, including assessments of effects of other intervention methods, involves the client or the client-surrogate in the planning of such programs, obtains the consent of the client, and respects the right of the client to terminate services at any time.

Behavior analysts base their programs on basic principles of behavior, use behavioral methods to evaluate their programs, and involve clients or their legal representatives in the planning of those programs. Behavior analysts inform clients of their right to end services at any time.

CASE EXAMPLE AND QUESTION 50: JERRY S.

Jerry S. was a BCABA who had previously worked for years as a massage therapist. One of the first cases he receives in a group home for developmentally-disabled adults involved a female client who would apparently "out of the blue" run down the hall and hit another client in the back. She would laugh and then go in her room and sit on her bed. Jerry felt that she was tense and that this was the cause of her bursts of unpredictable aggression. He wrote an informal program that involved shoulder rubs for this client following any such incident.

As Jerry's supervisor, how would you handle this situation?

APPROVING INTERVENTIONS (4.01)

The behavior analyst must obtain the client's or client-surrogate's approval in writing of the behavior intervention procedures before implementing them.

It is an obligation of the behavior analyst to gain the client's approval, in writing, before a program is begun.

CASE EXAMPLE AND QUESTION 51A: JUAN AND CARL

Juan, a newly certified CBA, has just started working in a privately-owned school for children with autism. He has been asked to work with Carl, a child who has been shrieking and slapping himself in the face. Juan arrived at the school after the previous CBA resigned. She left behind a functional analysis and a note that said a treatment plan was needed. Due to the self-injurious nature of the behavior, Juan wants to begin treatment immediately. He told the teacher he assumed the parents would be fine

*with this because they knew a functional assessment had been con-
ducted by the previous CBA.*

*Since the functional assessment has been completed, can Juan
begin the treatment?*

REINFORCEMENT/PUNISHMENT (4.02)

*The behavior analyst recommends reinforcement rather than punishment
whenever possible. If punishment procedures are necessary, the behavior
analyst always includes reinforcement procedures for alternative behavior
in the program.*

Behavior analysts have a bias in favor of the use of reinforcers in behavior change programs and against the use of punishment. In some
cases, where punishment is the only alternative, reinforcers for other
behaviors should always be included as part of the program.

CASE EXAMPLE AND QUESTION 51B: JUAN AND CARL

*From Case 51a, Juan decides that Carl's face-slapping is main-
tained by self-reinforcement and is serious enough to warrant a
punishment procedure as an intervention. When Carl slaps his
face, Juan wants Carl's hands to be firmly pulled away from his
face, and for the therapist to say in a loud voice, "No!"*

*What else does Juan need to do before submitting this program for
approval?*

AVOIDING HARMFUL REINFORCERS (4.03)

*The behavior analyst minimizes the use of items as potential reinforcers
that may be harmful to the long-term health of the client or participant*

(e.g., cigarettes, or sugar or fat-laden food), or that may require undesirably marked deprivation procedures as establishing operations.

Although some reinforcers may be quite effective for some clients, if those reinforcers could be harmful in the long-term, they should be avoided if at all possible. Behavior analysts should avoid the use of establishing (motivating) operations that involve significant degrees of deprivation.

CASE EXAMPLE AND QUESTION 52: MARK AND EDDIE

Mark was the CABA assigned to one house in a residential facility for verbal, ambulatory adults with moderate to severe mental retardation. He was supervised by a CBA who only came to the facility for an hour or so each week. Because of this, Mark was called on to draft most of the behavior programs and plan interventions. Eddie was an extremely active client who was constantly leaving whichever activity in which he was supposed to be involved. If he was scheduled to be in the house, he would leave and wander around the grounds. If Eddie was scheduled to be in the education building, he would often leave and go to his bedroom. Mark decided that because Eddie liked sweets, a good intervention would be to start reinforcing Eddie with candy or a small glass of Coke every ten minutes throughout the day if Eddie was where he was supposed to be.

Are there any special considerations for this reinforcement schedule that is so rich with unhealthy food?

ON-GOING DATA COLLECTION (4.04)

The behavior analyst collects data, or asks the client, client-surrogate, or designated others to collect data needed to assess progress within the program.

Behavior analysts always collect data and continue data collection to evaluate a program's effectiveness. The behavior analyst or some other designated person involved with the behavior program might do this.

CASE EXAMPLE AND QUESTION 53A:
MICHELLE AND DOUG

Michelle was the CBA who was working with Doug, a fourteen-year-old who was in a special education class for teenagers with emotional disorders. At home, Doug engaged in mild aggressive behaviors toward his younger brother which included pushing him or hitting him with a light slap. Doug's brother would yell and start to fight back. Doug's mother told Michelle that the behaviors were not severe enough to really hurt anyone, however, she was concerned that the intensity of the aggression could escalate if it wasn't stopped now. Michelle planned an intervention and sent detailed notes to Doug's mother about how to handle aggressive outbursts. Michelle told the mother she would call every week or so to see how things were going.

Is there anything else Michelle should have done?

PROGRAM MODIFICATIONS (4.05)

The behavior analyst modifies the program on the basis of data.

Behavior analysts are "online" with the programs they implement, which means that they continue to look at the data to determine if the program is working, and if necessary, make changes to the program to assure success.

CASE EXAMPLE AND QUESTION 53B:
MICHELLE AND DOUG

In Case 53a, Michelle was eventually prompted by her supervisor to implement treatment for the aggression in Doug's home. After two weeks of data collection, although Michelle was sure her intervention would be effective, the data showed that Doug's behavior was not improving.

The behavior program for aggression had been highly effective with other students.

Should Michelle just keep trying with this program? How long should she try before she changes to another approach?

PROGRAM MODIFICATIONS CONSENT (4.06)

The behavior analyst explains the program modifications and the reasons for the modifications to the client or client-surrogate and obtains consent to implement the modifications.

If it is necessary to make changes to the behavior program, the behavior analyst explains the reasons for the changes to the client or his or her legal representative, and receives consent for the changes.

CASE EXAMPLE AND QUESTION 54:
SHAKIRA AND TAWANA

Shakira is a CBA working in a special education classroom. Students spend part of the school day in the classroom and they are mainstreamed the remainder of the day. Tawana is a tall, lanky twelve-year-old who swears and becomes disruptive in class. She is on a behavior program that worked well until recently when the program became ineffective. Knowing her clients very well,

Shakira quickly figured out that Tawana was bored with the reinforcers. Shakira planned some changes in the intervention, including changing the reinforcers, reinforcement schedule, and adding consequences for misbehavior.

Because the behavior plan was already in effect, Shakira was certain that all of the permission forms that were previously signed would cover the new version of the program. Was she correct in assuming this?

LEAST RESTRICTIVE PROCEDURES (4.07)

The behavior analyst reviews and appraises the restrictiveness of alternative interventions and always recommends the least restrictive procedures likely to be effective in dealing with a behavior problem.

In determining alternatives in behavior programs, the behavior analyst will always try to use the least-restrictive method, which is, at the same time, still likely to be effective.

CASE EXAMPLE AND QUESTION 55:
DR. DAVID K. AND JASON

Jason, a ten-year-old with learning disabilities and social acting out, was mainstreamed into an elementary school physical education class. Jason would frequently disrupt the whole class with his antics. He would squeal loudly if he missed the ball and he would make every attempt to run in a humorous manner so that other students would laugh. The coach was frustrated and was ready to implement his own behavioral intervention that was to have Jason run around the track each time he misbehaved. The school principal sent Dr. David K., a BCBA, to meet with the coach and discuss alternatives. Dr. K. suggested that the first intervention simply be that when Jason acted out, he would be sent to the bench to sit and watch. Dr. K. explained to the coach that this was a procedure that was research-based and known to be effective.

Why else was "sit-and-watch" preferable to running around the track?

TERMINATION CRITERIA (4.08)

The behavior analyst establishes understandable and objective (i.e., measurable) criteria for the termination of the program and describes them to the client or client-surrogate.

At the onset of behavior programming, the behavior analyst will specify some criterion for determining when to end the program, for example, if the goal was to treat head-banging, the criterion might be zero incidents in a two-week period.

CASE EXAMPLE AND QUESTION 56A:
DR. JACK N. AND MRS. BAKER

Dr. Jack N. was consulting with clients who were senior citizens living in a residential facility. Mrs. Baker refused to walk anywhere. She sat in a wheelchair day after day and within a short period of time she no longer had the strength to walk to the dining room or down the hall. The medical staff identified walking as the number one goal for Mrs. Baker. Dr. N. knew that behavioral services for this activity would probably only be needed for a few weeks.

Should Dr. N. tell Mrs. Baker he will be working with her until she improves or should he wait until he is ready to terminate her services?

TERMINATING CLIENTS (4.09)

The behavior analyst terminates the relationship with the client when the established criteria for termination are attained, as in when a series of planned or revised intervention goals has been completed.

When the previously-established goal has been met, the behavior analyst will inform the client that behavioral services are no longer required and will close the case.

CASE EXAMPLE AND QUESTION 56B:
DR. JACK N. AND MRS. BAKER

In Case 56a, Dr. N. was exactly correct when he told the facility administrator he would have Mrs. Baker out of the wheelchair and walking again in record time. Dr. N. used very systematic shaping to add some distance to each day's walk. By the end of two months, Mrs. Baker could walk to the dining room using a cane. Dr. N. told Mrs. Baker she was ready to "graduate" and walk on her own. She began to say she didn't want Dr. N. to leave the facility. The more he thought about it, Dr. N decided he could expand and extend Mrs. Baker's walking program. He could try to get her to walk without the cane or to walk a greater distance, such as to the yard outside.

When a client is doing extremely well, is it a good idea to extend programming?

RESPONSES TO CASE QUESTION 50: JERRY S.

As Jerry's supervisor, you would first need to remind him that he is now a behavior analyst, and that it is time to leave massage therapy behind and begin thinking in terms of contingencies of reinforcement. It would appear that Jerry needs some on-the-job training on how to analyze cases like this one, including data collection. He will also need to be trained on the importance of working with the legal representatives of the clients, including their right to terminate services.

RESPONSES TO CASE QUESTION 51A: JUAN AND CARL

According to the Guidelines, Juan needs to obtain the client's or client-surrogate's (in this case, the parents) permission for the intervention procedures and could use this as an occasion to meet the parents.

RESPONSES TO CASE QUESTION 51B: JUAN AND CARL

Because behavior analysts should recommend reinforcement rather than punishment whenever possible, Carl's program needs to have some reinforcement procedures for alternative behaviors, such as holding and playing with a toy, raising his hand to get the teacher's attention, or using a musical instrument or art materials.

RESPONSES TO CASE QUESTION 52: MARK AND EDDIE

The Guidelines state that behavior analysts should minimize reinforcers that may be harmful to the health of the client. It is possible that this much sugar could have a negative effect on Eddie's blood sugar level. If Eddie was responsive to very small amounts of these reinforcers, such that at the end of the day, he had only received one half Coke and one half bag of M&Ms, this might be acceptable. Any food reinforcers would, of course, have to be approved by the medical staff and dietician. And, if this program was successful, Mark would want to stretch the schedule to fifteen-min, then twenty-min, and so on, so that the total amount of sugar per day was not excessive.

RESPONSES TO CASE QUESTION 53A:
MICHELLE AND DOUG

Whenever an intervention is implemented, data should be collected to evaluate the results of the intervention. It is appropriate for behavior analysts to train clients, professionals, and client surrogates (in this case, parents) to take data. Because Doug is aggressive in the home setting, the parents need to be taking data at home. The behavior analyst should design a data collection system and train the parents.

RESPONSES TO CASE QUESTION 53B:
MICHELLE AND DOUG

Behavior analysts must modify behavior programs on the basis of data, but what is not known, and which must be decided in each case, is how much data. When do you know when it is time to quit a procedure and try something different? This is a difficult question that certainly requires careful thought and input from experienced behavior analysts who understand the client and the setting where the behavior occurs. In this case, because the program has been successful with other students, we need to know more about those cases and the circumstances surrounding the assessment of effectiveness.

RESPONSES TO CASE QUESTION 54:
SHAKIRA AND TAWANA

When a behavior program is modified, the behavior analyst needs to explain the modifications and obtain consent again. In this case, consent would come from the parents. The changes should also be explained to Tawana.

RESPONSES TO CASE QUESTION 55:
DR. DAVID K. AND JASON

Because this is the first attempt at a behavior plan for Jason, the behavior analyst needs to start with the least restrictive procedures. "Sit-and-

watch," which is a brief time-out, is a better starting point than the physically grueling, and potentially dangerous, task of running around a track in
the hot sun.

RESPONSES TO CASE QUESTION 56A:
DR. JACK N. AND MRS. BAKER

*Dr. N. needs to establish criteria for the walking program and explain the
criteria to the facility administrator. He also needs to explain to Mrs. Baker,
in terms she can understand, that as soon she can walk a certain distance,
she will "graduate" from her walking program. If she has family members,
they should also be consulted on this matter.*

RESPONSES TO CASE QUESTION 56B:
DR. JACK N. AND MRS. BAKER

*In general, the behavior analyst needs to terminate the relationship when
the established criteria are obtained. In this case, if the administrator and
Mrs. Baker's family wished to further extend her goals, having Dr. N. stay
on the case a while longer would be appropriate.*

Chapter 8

The Behavior Analyst as Teacher or Supervisor (Guideline 5)

The majority of Board Certified Behavior Analysts® become supervisors within a short time after completing their graduate training. Training others to carry out behavioral procedures is an essential part of behavior analysis treatment because in most cases, the treatment occurs in the client's natural environment where these "significant others" are a large part of the client's life. A student who is referred for classroom behavior problems usually cannot be successfully treated in an off-campus counseling session that occurs after school. An effective treatment will involve observation in the classroom to determine controlling variables, and the teacher will most likely be involved in the behavior change program. The behavior analyst might observe that little Jenny is off-task during certain activities, that the other children reinforce it, and that the teacher contributes to the problem by providing unintentional intermittent attention. In this case, the behavior analyst's job consists of training the teacher how to increase the likelihood that Jenny will stay on task (perhaps by changing her class seating arrangement and her academic instruction level) and then additionally training the teacher to respond more systematically to the on-task, off-task behavior (Guideline 5.01). Basically, the teacher will be trained to be much better skilled in ignoring off-task behavior and watching for on-task behavior and immediately reinforcing it. It is entirely appropriate for the behavior analyst to train the teacher in this way because there is no "specialized training" involved. The teacher will have all the prerequisite skills and have the appropriate "scope of practice" for such an intervention. And, it should be made clear, that the behavior analyst in this case must operate within his or her level of expertise as well, that is, this behavior analyst has had special training working with children in schools and in training teachers.

It would not be appropriate for the behavior analyst to try and train playground aides in this same use of extinction and reinforcement (Guideline 5.02). Such personnel do not usually have a college degree and are not certified teachers. The underlying principle involved here is that behavior analysts do not train others to use behavioral procedures if there is some chance that they will be used inappropriately. A playground aide might be appropriately trained to take data on the effects of an intervention, but the actual program would need to be carried out by a certified teacher. A similar consideration has to be made in the case of behavioral treatments in residential facilities for individuals with developmental disabilities. The majority of staff members in these facilities have a high school degree and no advanced training. Our Guidelines are clear that training such staff in sophisticated behavioral procedures is inappropriate. These Guidelines are also clear that the behavior analyst is responsible for carrying out the training in the proper way and that proper follow-up supervision is also required (Guideline 5.09).

For BCBAs who become teachers or instructors, the Guidelines set a high standard as well. The behavior analyst is obligated to make clear what are the course objectives, requirements, and evaluation procedures (Guidelines 5.03, 5.04, 5.05), and further, to employ behavior analysis principles in teaching (Guideline 5.07). In addition, the behavior analyst must know at the outset whether the student (or supervisee) has the prerequisite skills for the course, and if not, he or she should be referred for remedial skill training (Guideline 5.08). There is a great deal of research on the use of behavioral procedures in teaching; we basically know how to design and execute very effective training for a wide variety of topic areas from preschool through graduate school. The BACB

Guidelines insist that these principles be employed with students and supervisees anywhere that "academic policies allow." This is good news for students because our research shows that the use of study objectives, frequent testing, prompt feedback, and active responding are all much preferred by students over traditional teaching methods that involve lectures followed by multiple choice midterm and final exams.

THE BEHAVIOR ANALYST AS TEACHER AND/OR SUPERVISOR (5.0)

Behavior analysts delegate to their employees, supervisees, and research assistants only those responsibilities that such persons can reasonably be expected to perform competently.

Behavior analysts must use good judgment when deciding whether they can pass on certain tasks to their employees or assistants. It certainly makes life easier to hand off certain, perhaps onerous or routine chores to others, but unless you know that the delegated person actually has the skills to accept these responsibilities, it is a risky decision. As a general rule, you would want to have actually seen the person perform the task on more than one occasion with close supervision before actually delegating certain responsibilities to him or her.

CASE EXAMPLE AND QUESTION 57: DR. Z.

Taking baseline data from videotapes seemed like such an easy task that Dr. Z. had no trouble making the decision to let his student Jessica take over this routine chore. He gave her a set of written definitions of the key behaviors, showed her the equipment, and let her begin working independently. About once a week, he would ask Jessica how it was going and she seemed enthused about her progress. Dr. Z. was on a plane on his way to a behavioral conference to present the data that Jessica had transcribed. He noticed something funny about the data. After a few minutes it dawned on him—she did not know the difference between whole interval and partial interval recording and would sometimes use one and sometimes the other.

Dr. Z. realized he should have been checking in on Jessica. What should he do about the conference presentation?

DESIGNING COMPETENT TRAINING PROGRAMS (5.01)

Behavior analysts who are responsible for education and training programs seek to ensure that the programs are competently designed, provide the proper experiences, and meet the requirements for licensure, certification, or other goals for which claims are made by the program.

It is the responsibility of the behavior analyst who is involved in education and training to make sure that courses are properly designed. Because we have a legacy from Skinner in the form of programmed instruction (Holland & Skinner, 1961), care in course design should be of utmost importance. Courses should provide the experiences necessary for teaching behavioral skills, not just lecturing to people, and they should meet licensure and certification requirements as per course descriptions.

LIMITATIONS ON TRAINING (5.02)

Behavior analysts do not teach the use of techniques or procedures that require specialized training, licensure, or expertise in other disciplines to individuals who lack the prerequisite training, legal scope of practice, or expertise, except as these techniques may be used in behavioral evaluation of the effects of various treatments, interventions, therapies, or educational methods.

We do not train assistants or paraprofessionals on behavioral procedures unless they have the necessary prerequisites; one exception is training assistants or others in data collection to help a qualified CBA evaluate the effects of treatment—this is allowed.

CASE EXAMPLE AND QUESTION 58A: DR. S.

Dr. S. was a CBA who worked for a company that owned seven group homes. Dr. S. was responsible for the behavior programming of all of the clients in the group homes, but he had CABAs and behavioral assistants to help him. Dr. S. was also responsible for arranging or providing training for all staff members who were CBAs and CABAs. Dr. S.'s supervisor, the company president, wanted to make sure all staff had the Continuing Education Unit's (CEU's) needed for recertification. She instructed Dr. S. to provide some CEU training. Because he was overloaded with work, Dr. S. arranged for the company's master's level psychometrist to do a daylong workshop on testing instead.

Are there any problems with this plan?

PROVIDING COURSE OBJECTIVES (5.03)

The behavior analyst provides a clear description of the objectives of a course, preferably in writing, at the beginning of the course.

Behavior analysts involved in teaching should provide a set of written objectives for the courses they teach. These will generally be quite specific as to exactly what behaviors the students have to engage in to earn a passing grade.

CASE EXAMPLE AND QUESTION 58B: DR. S.

In Case 58a, Dr. S.'s supervisor disapproved of his plan to have a nonbehavioral psychologist do a daylong workshop on testing. (She asked him what in the world he was thinking when he arranged this.) Dr. S. then arranged for a local chapter of the ABA to provide an all-day workshop on teaching behavioral skills to parents and foster parents. At the end of the training day, many of the staff came back to the group homes, found Dr. S. and told him that the workshop was the biggest waste of time they had ever seen. The speaker rambled from one thing to the next and at the end of the day, staff members felt like they'd learned nothing.

How could this have been prevented, and what, if anything, should be done about it now?

DESCRIBING COURSE REQUIREMENTS (5.04)

The behavior analyst provides a clear description of the demands of the course (e.g., papers, exams, projects) at the beginning of the course.

Behavior analysts involved in teaching should also provide a clear list of all course requirements at the onset of the course.

CASE EXAMPLE AND QUESTION 59A:
DR. NANCY P. AND GRETCHEN

Dr. Nancy P. was a university professor who taught a course in behavior analysis. Gretchen registered for Dr. P.'s class. Gretchen was a master's degree student who was interested in eventually getting certified as a CBA. She was also a single mother with a two-year old son. She worked part time as a behavior assistant in an elementary school and she was taking two university classes each semester. Dr. P. handed out the objectives for the course the first night of class. After reviewing the objectives, Gretchen clearly thought the class would be very beneficial. In the fourth week of classes, Gretchen felt as if she were drowning. There was a quiz in the class every week and she never dreamed so much study time would be required for this one class. In addition to the quizzes, the students had to write three papers and observe at least two therapy sessions. Gretchen went to see Dr. P. and told her she had never done poorly in a class but her quiz grades were sinking and she had no idea this was going to be so much work. Dr. P. was unsympa-

thetic, pointing out that she had handed out the objectives on the first night.

What should have been done differently in this case?

DESCRIBING EVALUATION REQUIREMENTS (5.05)

The behavior analyst provides a clear description of the requirements for the evaluation of student performance at the beginning of the course.

The behavior analyst who is involved in teaching should make clear to the students at the beginning of the course how they will be evaluated.

CASE EXAMPLE AND QUESTION 59B:
DR. NANCY P. AND GRETCHEN

In Case 59a, Gretchen somehow managed to struggle through the class. She wrote the papers, took the quizzes every week, and went to visit four therapy sessions rather than the required two sessions. Gretchen stayed up late and studied hard for the quizzes and she obtained near-perfect scores on the remaining exams. Gretchen put extra effort into her papers, finding additional references that were not required, and she took great care when documenting her therapy visits for Dr. P. By going beyond the call of duty, Gretchen was hoping for an "A" in the course. Gretchen was trying to get some financial assistance for graduate school and her grade point average was very important to her. Imagine her shock when she checked her grades online, only to discover that she was given a "C" in the course. Gretchen immediately went to see Dr. P. and tearfully explained that she had never received a "C" in her life.

Once again, Dr. P. was unmoved and said that the quizzes had accounted for seventy percent of the grade.

PROVIDING FEEDBACK TO STUDENTS/SUPERVISEES (5.06)

The behavior analyst provides feedback regarding the performance of a student or supervisee as frequently as the conditions allow.

Because research has shown that frequent feedback can improve motivation, learning, and performance, the behavior analyst should strive to provide to provide feedback as often as possible. Generally speaking, this feedback should closely follow the performance. If students take an exam every two weeks, they should receive feedback as soon as the exams are passed back, for example.

CASE EXAMPLE AND QUESTION 60:
DR. ANDY M. AND TARA

Dr. Andy M., a CBA who taught at the university and did private consulting, was supervising Tara, a graduate student in psychology. Tara, a CABA, was assigned to two middle school classrooms where she worked with adolescents who had behavior problems. After not seeing Dr. M. for at least three months, Tara received a phone call from him. He told Tara the teachers were not happy with her work and he was very sorry to tell her that she would probably lose her placement at the school.

What is the most ethical response for Dr. M. in this case? What should Tara have done before and after she got the phone call?

PROVIDING BEHAVIOR ANALYSIS PRINCIPLES IN TEACHING (5.07)

The behavior analyst utilizes as many principles of behavior analysis in teaching a course as the material, conditions, and academic policies allow.

The ethical behavior analyst who is involved in teaching should make ample use of the many principles of behavior in teaching.

These might include using study objectives, frequent quizzing, point systems, active learning, and so on.

CASE EXAMPLE AND QUESTION 61: DR. BENJAMIN Y.

Dr. Benjamin Y. is a CBA who teaches a university course on behavior analysis. University students take his course as well as community behavior analysts who are working on earning CBA certification. Dr. Y. is a brilliant man and is recognized nationally as an expert in the field of behavior analysis. However, he can be very sarcastic whenever a student asks a question and he presents the material as if everyone in the class is a doctoral student. There is one final exam at the end of Dr. Y.'s class that is the only basis for the course grade. Dr. Y. believes that as long as he is technically competent and knows the material well, his teaching methods are his choice.

Is Dr. Y. correct on this?

REQUIREMENTS OF SUPERVISEES (5.08)

The behavior analyst's behavioral requirements of a supervisee must be in the behavioral repertoire of the supervisee. If the behavior required is not in the supervisee's repertoire, the behavior analyst attempts to provide the conditions for the acquisition of the required behavior, and refers the supervisee for remedial skill development services, or provides them with such services, permitting them to meet at least minimal behavioral performance requirements.

When the behavior analyst is serving in the capacity of supervisor, it is important to know that the person supervised is actually capable of certain expected behaviors. If the person does not have the skill set, it is the responsibility of the behavior analyst supervisor to provide training on the necessary skills or refer the person to someone else who is qualified to do the training.

CASE EXAMPLE AND QUESTION 62: KATHY E.

Kathy E. was a CBA in a school system who supervised behavioral assistants and CABAs. In a meeting with three of the behavioral assistants, Kathy distributed the names of several children who had been recently referred for behavioral services. Kathy instructed the nondegreed behavioral assistants to go and observe the children on the list and "Come back with some baseline data." One of the behavioral assistants spoke up and told Kathy she didn't know how to do this. Kathy said, "It's not that hard people. We need to get it done—just do the best you can."

Was Kathy E. acting ethically in this situation?

TRAINING AND SUPERVISION (5.09)

Behavior analysts provide proper training and supervision to their employees or supervisees and take reasonable steps to see that such persons perform services responsibly, competently, and ethically. If institutional policies, procedures, or practices prevent fulfillment of this obligation, behavior analysts attempt to modify their role or to correct the situation to the extent feasible.

As discussed earlier, it is essential that behavior analysts take seriously the job of training their employees and those they supervise, for it is precisely these individuals, in all likelihood, who will actually be carrying out the treatment. Training is one are that is a real strength for behavior analysts because there has been so much research that has been done demonstrating empirically what are the most effective methods. To do anything other than competency-based training is considered taboo in most behavioral circles. Many behavior analysts will not only require that supervisees or employees demonstrate competence but also that they are fluent on the important tasks set out for them. Given this emphasis on effective training, behavior analysts should always attempt to optimize the contingencies in whatever setting they are working to provide the highest quality training.

CASE EXAMPLE AND QUESTION 63: BRODIE

Brodie just completed his master's degree in behavior analysis and was excited about his first job working for a small consulting firm. He was assigned to work with teachers setting up model classrooms, based on token economies, for behaviorally-disabled fifth graders in five schools in the county. He read all the research that was available, worked hard gathering up the materials he would need, and set up a training schedule that involved short modular presentations, followed by role playing, followed by actual demonstrations in a practice classroom. It would take at least a week, in his estimation. Brodie was shocked to find out that he would be given half a day at the quarterly in-service that was coming up.

If you were Brodie, what would you do next?

FEEDBACK TO SUPERVISEES (5.10)

The behavior analyst provides feedback to the supervisee in a way that increases the probability that the supervisee will benefit from the feedback.

There are many ways to provide feedback including verbal, written, and graphic feedback. Research suggests that feedback, which is descriptive and positive, for example, is more effective than that which is simply categorical ("Your performance was poor").

CASE EXAMPLE AND QUESTION 64: MARGO AND TIM

Margo, a seasoned PhD behavior analyst, had been supervising new CBAs and CABAs for years. Thus, it came as something of a surprise when one of her new charges didn't respond to some feedback that she gave him. It had been her custom for several years that new recruits got their feedback individually in short meetings about every two weeks. This would go on for about six months and then she would shift them to feedback once a month. For this young man, he just didn't seem to get the idea that he was to carry out certain specific tasks, check them off on a card that Margo provided, and then bring the card to supervision meetings. Tim would sit passively as she spoke to him, not nodding or smiling or asking any questions. At the end of the session, he would smile politely, say "Thank you," and leave.

Where would you go next with Tim?

REINFORCING SUPERVISEE BEHAVIOR (5.11)

The behavior analyst uses positive reinforcement as frequently as the behavior of the supervisee and the environmental conditions allow.

As a field, we stress the importance of positive reinforcement in our behavioral interventions, so it makes sense for the ethical behavior analyst to use positive reinforcement as often as possible with those they supervise.

CASE EXAMPLE AND QUESTION 65: STEVE L.

Steve L. was a CBA who supervised behavioral services in a large residential facility. A new CABA was working with a client who had some inappropriate social skills and episodes of aggression.

The CABA came to a meeting and presented her ideas for teaching the client how to behave more appropriately. In front of the entire treatment team, Steve said, "That is a dumb idea—it would never work. You are out to lunch if you think you can change a behavior like this using only praise." Most of the treatment team agreed with Steve's assessment of the proposed intervention, but they were appalled by his method of delivering feedback.

Someone needs to talk to Steve. Where would you start?

RESPONSES TO CASE QUESTION 57: DR. Z.

Dr. Z. paid severely for his misjudgment about Jessica. He had to apologize about having no data to present and didn't even try to explain how this happened to his colleagues. It was sufficiently embarrassing that he is unlikely to make this mistake again.

RESPONSES TO CASE QUESTION 58A: DR. S.

For CBAs and CABAs, training needs to be done by a person who is a CBA; the psychologist was not qualified to do CEU training for behavior analysts. Further, testing is an area that requires specialized training and supervision. The only exception to this would be a workshop that was designed to simply familiarize participants with testing procedures. Six hours of "familiarization" would probably be excessive, and in the case of these CBAs and CABAs, they would be better off earning CEU's. If Dr. S. cannot do the training, he should find another CBA.

RESPONSES TO CASE QUESTION 58B: DR. S.

Dr. S. should have received a clear description of the course objectives from the workshop leader. He then would have known if the information that was to be presented would be helpful to his staff. Unfortunately, there are some behavior analysts and workshop leaders who need better instruc-

*tional, organizational skills and more professional public speaking skills.
Dr. S. could ask his staff to fill out evaluations and those could be provided
to the workshop leader. If there was anything that was really outrageous, he
could give feedback to the certification board who approved the workshops.*

RESPONSES TO CASE QUESTION 59A:
DR. NANCY P. AND GRETCHEN

*Handing out course objectives is not enough. Dr. P. should have also pro-
vided the students with a clear description of all the requirements of the
course. When not provided with this, Gretchen should have asked for it. If
Gretchen had known what all was involved, she may have chosen to take the
class at another time.*

RESPONSES TO CASE QUESTION 59B:
DR. NANCY P. AND GRETCHEN

*The Guidelines state that behavior analysts who teach or supervise others
should provide a clear description for evaluating student performance at
the beginning of the course. On the first night of class, the students should
have received a written point-system or another method of explaining not
only what the course requirements were but also how much weight would be
given to each. After some soul searching, Gretchen went to the department
chairperson to complain.*

RESPONSES TO CASE QUESTION 60:
DR. ANDY M. AND TARA

*If Tara was engaging in unprofessional behaviors such as showing up late,
being rude to other professionals, or refusing to do work she had been assigned, her removal from the school may be warranted. However, if the
problem is that she was technically weak and needed more training, then
the issue here is with Dr. M. Behavior analysts who accept the responsibility
of supervising others need to provide the student (or supervisee) with feed-*

back. To do this effectively, Dr. M. cannot go three months or more without observing or meeting with Tara and shaping her performance; in fact, he should be meeting with her at least one hr per week to provide her feedback and training as necessary, including feedback from the teachers. If this had been done, Tara likely would have made the necessary adjustments to her behavior early on so that the teachers were satisfied with her performance.

RESPONSES TO CASE QUESTION 61: DR. BENJAMIN Y.

The Guidelines say that behavior analysts should use as many behavior analysis principles in teaching a course as the material, conditions, and policies allow. Dr. Y. should be providing students with reinforcement rather than sarcasm, he should be using principles such as shaping to break down the material so it is understandable, and he should be giving regular feedback to students through the use of smaller, more frequent quizzes, and so forth.

RESPONSES TO CASE QUESTION 62: KATHY E.

The behavior analyst who is a supervisor (Kathy) can only require work in the behavioral repertoire of those individuals who are being supervised. Before requiring behavioral assistants to do something like take a baseline, Kathy would need to provide training on this task. It would be more appropriate for behavioral assistants to receive the training and then work at the side of a CBA or CABA doing reliability observations, and so forth.

RESPONSES TO CASE QUESTION 63: BRODIE

Brodie should have clarified the time that he would be given for training on the front end of his assignment. It's a little too late to do anything about the time that he is allotted, but his only choice, other than quitting, is to greatly scale down his expectations for this first session. Rather than being competency-based, it will need to be an overview of token economies. As challenging as it might sound, his next step is to work with his consulting firm and lobby for the time needed to accomplish his overall task of actually setting up these token economies. One option is to work with each of the teachers individually and do them one at a time.

RESPONSES TO CASE QUESTION 64: MARGO AND TIM

Margo may be dealing with someone who does not take feedback well from a woman, regardless of her status. She will probably need to shorten the intervals between sessions to perhaps once a day or once every other day for a while. Margo will need to focus on specific behaviors that she can actually observe and record and make a graph of Tim's performance and require him to graph his performance as well. Other solutions may come to mind as you consider this case and we urge you to explore them as possibilities.

RESPONSES TO CASE QUESTION 65: STEVE L.

The Guidelines say that behavior analysts give feedback in a way that will help the supervisee benefit from the feedback. Positive reinforcement is used as frequently as possible with supervisees. Steve could say something like, "I see you've given this a lot of thought. I really appreciate you doing all this work before you came to the meeting. One concern I have is that this behavior often requires consequences and positive reinforcement ... how about if we modified your plan like this ...?"

Chapter 9

The Behavior Analyst
and the Workplace (Guideline 6)

Behavior analysts have been active in the workplace since the early 1970s. Behavior analysis in business and industry is known as Organizational Behavior Management (OBM) or Performance Management (PM). This special field has demonstrated that basic principles of behavior can be applied successfully in the business arena to produce happier, more productive employees (Daniels, 2000; Daniels & Daniels, 2004; Frederiksen, 1982; O'Brien, Dickinson, & Rosow, 1982). Guideline 6.0 requires the behavior analyst working in business and industry to be "adequately prepared" to consult in these organizations (Guideline 6.03). This means that consultants in business and industry must have had the necessary coursework and practicum supervision before offering their services in settings where the bottom line is important. As in any setting, the principles of behavior could be misused, probably to the disadvantage of workers rather than management, because management hires most consultants. Our Guidelines require behavior analysts to develop interventions that (a) are well thought out (Guideline 6.02), (b) benefit both employees as well as management (Guideline 6.04), and (c) "enhance the well being of employees." This latter condition shows an awareness that it would be quite easy to put employees at risk. For example, an unethical consultant could develop new schedules of reinforcement that would dramatically boost efficiency. Under some circumstances, much higher rates of performance could result in increased stress or injuries. In addition, there is warranted concern that the misuse of behavioral procedures could cause a backlash by employees and leave a bad taste in the mouth of management about behavior analysis.

Another feature of this Guideline is that it stresses a more common ethical standard about employment in general. That is, behavior analysts, like other professionals, have an obligation to adhere to job commitments (Guideline 6.01). If you sign a two-year contract with an organization, you are expected to stay with that company for the full two-year period. Or, if your contract includes a "noncompete clause," it is only ethical for you to abide by this restriction should you leave the firm. To break your contract and go into competition with your former employer is doubly unethical and likely to result in censure from your colleagues and a potential lawsuit as well.

One final ethical issue is covered in this Guideline. This has to do with a potential conflict between your commitment to these BACB® Guidelines and your employer. The most likely problem is that someone in your organization will ask you to do something "unethical" according to our standards. This might involve an apparently innocuous act of signing some paperwork indicating that you approve a behavior program when you do not, or to indicate that you have carried out some training for which you were not involved. Organizations, particularly in human services, come under periodic review from state or Federal agencies and discover, on short notice, that they are deficient on certain critical standards. Many of these involve documentation of client records indicating that clients have been assessed, that treatments have been provided, or that certain goals have been met. All of this usually requires the signature of the BCBA®, who attests to these facts—or not. Pressure on you to "cooperate" could be intense, but to comply would clearly be a violation of our ethical standards. Guideline 6.06 urges you to seek resolution of such conflicts without violating your adherence to the ethical principles of our field.

THE BEHAVIOR ANALYST AND THE WORKPLACE (6.0)

The behavior analyst adheres to job commitments, assesses employee inter-actions before intervention, works within his/her scope of training, develops interventions that benefit employees, and resolves conflicts within these Guidelines.

JOB COMMITMENTS (6.01)

The behavior analyst adheres to job commitments made to the employing organization.

Behavior analysts are not different from other professionals when it comes to job commitments: The rule is, you follow through with your agreements.

CASE EXAMPLE AND QUESTION 66: JOANNE

Joanne was a PhD level CBA who accepted a new job working for a large behavioral consulting firm. Joanne signed an employment contract stating that she would stay with the company at least two years and that she would work a minimum of twenty-hr billable per week. The consulting firm spent two months training Joanne. Joanne began work and quickly decided she did not want to work twenty hours each week. Without telling anyone, she dropped her caseload so that she was working twelve to fifteen hours weekly. Then, after only six months on the job, Joanne accepted an offer for more money with a competing company.

What are the Guidelines violations here?

ASSESSING EMPLOYEE INTERACTIONS (6.02)

The behavior analyst assesses the behavior-environment interactions of the employees before designing behavior analytic programs.

Behavior analysts consulting in business settings are often asked to find ways of improving performance. The most direct way may be through changes in the way that employees are paid or in the use of disincentives for poor performance. However, we should not lose sight of the fact that some consistently less-than-stellar behavior may be due to the physical environment itself. Employees who work in settings where the equipment is in need of repair, where it is loud and noisy, or where there are safety issues, should not be faulted for their performance. The ethical behavior analyst always takes these environmental factors into account and brings these issues to the attention of management for correction before proposing solutions involving contingencies of reinforcement.

CASE EXAMPLE AND QUESTION 67: DR. BILL R.

Dr. Bill R., a BCBA, was assigned to work in four 16-bed houses in a residential facility. Dr. R. started this new placement by going to the houses, reviewing client folders, and taking the clients who needed behavior programs to a training room so he could get to know them. Dr. R. figured he would spend the first few weeks getting programs written, data sheets designed, and any assessments that needed to be done completed. Two weeks later, he showed up at one house to train the staff on a behavior program. While he waited for a shift supervisor to gather staff members together, Dr. R. asked one staff person if she had worked on any behavior programs with clients. She said, "Well, that other fella who was here asked us to take data all day long. I'm telling you, we don't have time for all that garbage!" Dr. R. continued to wait because some staff members had not returned from lunch on time. Every so of-

ten, one particular staff member would go to a client who needed to do an activity that was scheduled. In a very loud, threatening, and negative voice, this staff member would bark out an order such as, "Richard, I told you it was time to get ready. You better get up outta here and get dressed before that bus gets here. I'm not tellin' you again."

Do the Guidelines offer any advice that could have helped Dr. R.?

PREPARING FOR CONSULTATION (6.03)

The behavior analyst implements or consults on behavior management programs for which the behavior analyst has been adequately prepared.

It would simply be unethical for a behavior analyst to consult in any business setting unless he or she was properly trained for the task. There are enough differences between business or industrial settings and typical human services settings that special preparation is necessary.

CASE EXAMPLE AND QUESTION 68: FREDERICK

Frederick's next-door neighbor was the general manager of a hardware store that was part of a nationally recognized chain. Frederick, a BCBA, specialized in the design of sheltered workshops for the physically handicapped. One day at a community barbecue, the neighbor began telling Frederick about some performance problems of his employees. He said the employees came to work late, showed no initiative, and their customer service skills left much to be desired. Because Frederick encountered these same problems in his workshops, he began offering suggestions.

What might be a more appropriate response from Frederick?

EMPLOYEES INTERVENTIONS (6.04)

The behavior analyst develops interventions that benefit the employees as well as management.

Consultants in business settings are almost always hired by management to solve performance problems that affect the bottom line of the company. As a behavior analyst, you should at the same time make sure that any interventions you propose will also work to the advantage of the employees.

CASE EXAMPLE AND QUESTION 69: SHARON P.

Sharon P. felt she was very lucky to be working for one of the largest business-consulting firms in the country. Although it was not exactly behaviorally oriented, she was allowed to work on special projects that involved company mergers. The opportunities for using behavioral solutions were enormous and Sharon felt good about the contribution she was making, until the day that she was assigned to an oil rig in the Gulf of Mexico. She would work two weeks straight, living in a nicely-appointed cubicle on the rig, and then get a week off. Her assignment was to figure out how to increase the productivity of the 153 workers by nine percent to at least 1.9 million barrels a day of crude oil. Currently they were rated the lowest of any of the southern-sector platforms with a score of eighty-five percent efficiency. Each one-percent deficit was costing the company 2.5 million dollars per year and Sharon was under intense pressure from the company president to find a solution. After three months, she came up with a plan that involved an intermittent schedule of reinforcement which would increase the efficiency of the "roughnecks" and "roustabouts" (roughnecks and roustabouts are the names for specific oil rig jobs; these are not intended to be derogatory terms for workers). Basically, she was proposing to have them earn daily and weekly bonuses for in-

creased production without increased accidents. If they could meet the goals, they would increase their daily salaries from $300 to $350 per day, which Sharon deemed the minimum necessary to get this boost in productivity.

The company president liked Sharon's plan but said that $50 per day was ridiculous. Should she go back to the drawing board for a new plan?

EMPLOYEE HEALTH AND WELL BEING (6.05)

The behavior analyst develops interventions that enhance the health and well being of the employees.

It is not difficult to devise ingenious schedules of reinforcement that will motivate employees to be more productive; the concern is that this might, at the same time, put them at risk for illness or injury. Working faster could easily lead to taking short cuts or ignoring safety standards that are designed to prevent employees from injuring themselves.

CASE EXAMPLE AND QUESTION 70: PETER B.

Peter B. received his PhD in Industrial/Organizational psychology and was quickly hired by a large online retailer to improve productivity. His directive was to find ways of increasing the work-output of employees in the shipping department. After making informal observations over a three-week period, Peter recommended that the company institute a pay-for-performance system that would reward employees for picking up the pace of work, learning to pack the boxes more quickly, and take fewer steps in doing so. His estimate was that overall output could be increased by at least fifteen percent, with only a two percent payroll increase because of the way the pay would be contingent on performance. A

CBA working in the Human Resources Department got wind of this proposal and asked to review it before it was put in place.

Why might the CBA be interested?

CONFLICTS WITH ORGANIZATIONS (6.06)

If the demands of an organization with which behavior analysts are affiliated conflict with these Guidelines, behavior analysts clarify the nature of the conflict, make known their commitment to these Guidelines, and to the extent feasible, seek to resolve the conflict in a way that permits the fullest adherence to these Guidelines.

It should be apparent from this Guideline that behavior analysts take their ethics seriously, even to the point of letting others know of our high standards and that we feel the need to resolve any conflict between these Guidelines and other work-related demands.

CASE EXAMPLE AND QUESTION 71: HEATHER

A company owning several residential facilities and group homes was getting ready to undergo a federal review. As soon as the administrators heard that the review team was coming, they went into their hysterical mode. Heather was a CBA who worked in the facilities. In preparation for the review, Heather was instructed by one administrator to "… get over there to those houses, get some assessments written up, write some behavior programs, and make sure there is some data. You may have to backdate some of it if necessary." Heather was nervous about this because she was an honest person and she had not been given the opportunity to spend time with these clients.

Assuming that she wishes to use professional language, what should Heather say to the administrator?

RESPONSES TO CASE QUESTION 66: JOANNE

Joanne agreed to stay with the company for two years and she left after six months. She signed a contract and clearly is in violation of the Guidelines and her contract. The Guidelines say that behavior analysts adhere to their job commitments. Joanne should have worked the promised twenty hours per week unless a schedule change was mutually agreed on by the consulting firm. Sometimes, things happen in life so that one cannot honor a commitment (e.g., a behavior analyst feels the need to relocate to be with a dying parent). In these cases, the behavior analyst should make every attempt to work with the employer to arrange a smooth transition.

RESPONSES TO CASE QUESTION 67: DR. BILL R.

The Guidelines state that behavior analysts should assess the behavior-environment interactions of the employees before designing behavior analytic programs. Dr. R. would have a smoother start if he knew what he was dealing with in terms of staff attitudes and behavior before trying to implement detailed or sophisticated programs.

RESPONSES TO CASE QUESTION 68: FREDERICK

As exciting as it might be to expand his consulting from sheltered workshops to big-time businesses, Frederick needs to reflect on his lack of experience and training in this area and recommend that his neighbor contact a person trained in PM or perhaps direct him to a consulting firm that does this sort of work routinely.

RESPONSES TO CASE QUESTION 69: SHARON P.

According to the Guidelines, Sharon did the right thing in proposing a pay-for-performance system that would benefit management (they stood to make millions) and the oil rig workers as well. She now has an ethical dilemma that may result in her refusing to work on the oil rig contract for her consulting firm. Her position was that it was unethical for her to design a system that got the roughnecks and roustabouts to work harder without their earning any increased compensation for such difficult and dangerous work.

RESPONSES TO CASE QUESTION 70: PETER B.

CBAs are required to follow these Guidelines, but in this case, the industrial psychologist would not need to adhere to them. Certainly any time there is an increase in productivity there is some chance that this involves employees working faster or possibly cutting corners to earn the performance bonus. Both situations might put them at some risk for injury and someone needs to ask questions about the safety and well-being of the employees. The CBA was correct in raising questions in this case.

RESPONSES TO CASE QUESTION 71: HEATHER

The administrator is engaging in serious unethical conduct. Heather needs to show her the Guidelines and tell her she will do her best to assess the situation and work within the Guidelines to make any program improvements she can before the review team arrives. If the administrator persists, Heather should reply with the following: "Please don't ask me to violate my professional ethics." Should the administrator not back down, Heather may need to consider employment with a more ethical organization.

Chapter 10

The Behavior Analyst
and Research (Guideline 7)

Conducting research in behavior analysis involves the most complex set of requirements that can be found in these BACB® Guidelines. Some are quite broad and include planning your research in such a way that the findings will not be misused by others (Guideline 7.0 [a]) and be ethically acceptable by other researchers and presumably consumers as well (Guideline 7.0 [e]). Others require the behavior analyst researcher to attend to the fine details of debriefing (Guideline 7.11) and paying participants (Guideline 7.17). In the most general sense, this Guideline makes it clear that "do no harm" is certainly the watchword of the applied behavioral researcher (Guideline 7.01 [b]), whether it involves carefully supervising assistants (Guideline 7.0 [b]), obtaining informed consent (Guideline 7.04), or later in the process, using the findings for instructive purposes (Guideline 7.02). Of course, the best protection against harming participants is to always seek advanced approval of your local Institutional Review Board (IRB; Guideline 7.0 [e]) and guidance via peer consultation when designing your study; it goes without saying that behavioral researchers will comply with state and Federal law (Guideline 7.03), obtain informed consent from participants (Guideline 7.04), and inform them of how the data will be used (Guideline 7.06). It is in the best interest of the behavior analysis researcher and the field if participants are not only spared any harm but also treated as well as possible while they are involved in any experiment (or therapy). Because most applied behavioral research is conducted in the participant's environment, the researcher has an obligation to avoid interfering as much as possible and to only collect the data necessary for the study (Guideline 7.07). Participants should be ensured anonymity (Guideline 7.09), informed that they can withdraw at any time (Guideline 7.10), and debriefed at the conclusion of the study (Guideline 7.11). Most behavioral research does not involve any deception, but, if it is essential for the conduct of the study, and there are no alternatives, it is permissible as long it does not involve any physical risk or adverse emotional experience (Guideline 7.05 [a–c]). Behavior analysts using animals in their research must comply with the Federal Animal Welfare Act (1990) and assure that the animals are treated humanely (Guideline 7.20).

It is a common courtesy, and also a Guideline, that once the research is concluded and is being written for publication, the behavioral researcher will acknowledge those who helped with the study (Guideline 7.15) and pay particular attention to the issue of who receives publication credit (Guideline 7.16).

THE BEHAVIOR ANALYST AND RESEARCH (7.0)

Behavior analysts design, conduct, and report research in accordance with recognized standards of scientific competence and ethical research. Behavior analysts conduct research with human and non-human research participants according to the proposal approved by the local human research committee, and Institutional Review Board.

Behavior analysts involved in research must be specially trained to high standards of proficiency and conduct themselves in an ethical fashion. They must have a proposed plan of research, which is then submitted to an IRB or other local human research committee (e.g., educational research must be approved by the local school board research committee). Further, ethical behavior analysts must follow the plan once it is approved.

CASE EXAMPLE AND QUESTION 72A: RON

Ron was a CABA who was a graduate student. As a part of the Psychology Department's training, Ron had a part-time position to provide behavioral services in two middle schools. This work was closely supervised by a BCBA. A real believer in the potential of behavior analysis to make a difference in society, Ron was also interested in behavioral analytic research in a wide variety of areas, including behavioral safety, PM, and behavioral sports psychology. He wanted to be a researcher and was very eager to get published. Ron played tennis in high school and he felt that he could help the tennis team increase their frequency of wins. Ron approached the tennis coach and asked if he could do some research to improve the performance of tennis team members. Because this was not an official psychology departmental assignment for Ron, he told the coach he was going to be "Flexible to the max, sort of making this up as I go along, you know, rolling with the punches," and he hoped the coach understood the need to be flexible. Ron figured that as the weeks progressed, the interventions he needed to implement would become more apparent.

The coach did give his permission for Ron to do the research and work with the team. Were any other approvals needed?

(a) Behavior analysts plan their research so as to minimize the possibility that results will be misleading.

A great deal of planning goes into research, and one goal is to assure that when the results are obtained, they are truthful.

CASE EXAMPLE AND QUESTION 72B: RON

In Case 72a, Ron's major professor heard about this research project. Ron finally got on track, writing the proposal, getting approval, and detailing the proposed interventions. Ron was taking data throughout the study and he had observers taking data when he was unavailable. It came time to write the results. One method of graphing the data showed absolutely no effect of the interventions on the performance of tennis team members. If Ron used certain statistical tests or presented only the data from a few participants, the results appeared to be a little better. Ron felt that he owed it to the coach and players to present the data in the most positive manner possible.

Is there any problem with selecting a method of data presentation that shows the research in the most positive way possible?

(b) Behavior analysts conduct research competently and with due concern for the dignity and welfare of the participants. Researchers and assistants are permitted to perform only those tasks for which they are appropriately trained and prepared.

It is expected that behavior analysts will be proficient in carrying out their research and that uppermost in their considerations will be the safety and well-being of the participants.

CASE EXAMPLE AND QUESTION 73

Several years ago, some research was conducted on teaching safety skills to elementary school children. In this research, the children were taught to cross the street safely after school. As one can imagine, during the baseline phase in a study like this, observers might be watching children who crossed the street without looking both ways or who engaged in other unsafe behaviors.

What rules are necessary during the baseline phase?

(c) Behavior analysts are responsible for the ethical conduct of research conducted by them or by others under their supervision or control.

Behavior analysts involved in research must remember that they are responsible for all of those involved on the research team including observers, therapists, or data analysts.

CASE EXAMPLE AND QUESTION 74:
DR. YUNG-HA C. AND KIRSTEN

Dr. Yung-Ha C. was a CBA who taught in a university psychology program. Dr. C. was conducting research in a school that dealt with the effects of teacher approval and prompts on student behavior. In this study, teachers were cued by observers when it was time to reinforce children for target behaviors. Dr. C. trained undergraduate students on the observation system. He met with them in his office as a group one time per week to talk about the progress of the study. In addition, a graduate student had trained a teacher aide to take the data and serve as a reliability observer. Several weeks into the study, one of the undergraduate observers complained to Dr. C. about Kirsten, the teacher aide who was taking data. Kirsten apparently did not like one child in the study and was not giving the teacher the cues to reinforce this child. Sometimes, when sitting with a reliability observer at her side, Kirsten would make fun of the teacher's poor teaching, muttering under her breath, "That was just brilliant, just brilliant ... why don't you let that kid run the class?"

If you were Dr. C., what would you do?

(d) Behavior analysts conducting applied research conjointly with provision of clinical or human services obtain required external reviews of proposed clinical research and observe requirements for both intervention and research involvement by client-participants.

Behavioral researchers in clinical, educational, or rehabilitative settings will have their research proposals approved by the clinic, school, or hospital where they want to work and also by relevant external review committees (i.e., IRB).

CASE EXAMPLE AND QUESTION 75: CARL

Carl was a CABA who was working on his master's degree in psychology. He wanted to do research in a high school that was in a low-income neighborhood. He began volunteering at the school and he established an excellent working relationship with the principal and some of the teachers. When it came time to start his study, Carl provided each of his committee members with a prospectus. He met with the school and got the approvals to conduct his research. He sent an email to everyone on his committee saying that he had obtained "approvals to start his study."

Was Carl ready to begin his research after obtaining approvals from the school principal and the teachers involved in the study?

(e) In planning research, behavior analysts consider its ethical acceptability under these Guidelines. If an ethical issue is unclear, behavior analysts seek to resolve the issue through consultation with institutional review boards, animal care and use committees, peer consultations, or other proper mechanisms.

The Guidelines describe in detail the ethical requirements for behavior analyst researchers. If you have any question about an ethical issue, you should contact the relevant committees or IRB to seek a resolution before the research begins.

CASE EXAMPLE AND QUESTION 76: SHONDRA

Shondra was a CBA who had all of the necessary approvals to begin her research with young children at a neighborhood community center. Shondra had her committee members sign off on the research, the community center's director had approved the study, and she had IRB approval. To get the IRB and committee approvals, Shondra submitted a detailed prospectus outlining her plans for both the baseline and intervention phases of her study. Shondra's research was designed to evaluate the effectiveness of token reinforcers. Children could earn tokens that could be exchanged for small, inexpensive toys. After beginning her study, Shondra noticed that the toys were the source of some unethical conduct on the part of the teachers. The teachers were very much aware of which children in the program came from low-income homes and which children were middle class. The teachers began systematically discriminating against the children who they perceived did not need the toys. Shondra's study had gone awry.

What is her next move?

SCHOLARSHIP AND RESEARCH (7.01)

(a) The behavior analyst engaged in study and research is guided by the conventions of the science of behavior including the emphasis on the analysis of individual behavior and strives to model appropriate applications in professional life.

Behavior analyst researchers conduct their research in the tradition of Skinner's (1953) model of operant conditioning and emulate this practice in their occupation.

CASE EXAMPLE AND QUESTION 77: BRUCE

Bruce was a CBA and a graduate student who worked in a residential DD facility for ambulatory, verbal adults. He supervised two houses that each had sixteen clients. As a hobby, Bruce loved music. He played in a small band and he listened to many types of music. Bruce decided that as a part of his behavioral programming responsibilities, he would do a research project that evaluated the effects of music therapy on his clients. He would play music in the houses for an hour each day, keeping a record of the type of music played. Then, at the end of the hour, Bruce would ask the clients how the music made them feel.

Bruce was surprised when his behavioral colleagues were not so impressed with this idea. What was the problem?

(b) Behavior analysts take reasonable steps to avoid harming their clients, research participants, students, and others with whom they work, and to minimize harm where it is foreseeable and unavoidable. Harm is defined here as negative effects or side effects of behavior analysis that outweigh positive effects in the particular instance, and that are behavioral or physical and directly observable.

Do no harm: Researchers do everything they can to make sure that experimental participants are not injured in any way in the course of a study. Behavior analysts are particularly concerned that any negative effects are in all cases outweighed by the benefits of the study to the participant.

CASE EXAMPLE AND QUESTION 78: DR. SAM H.

Dr. Sam H. is a BCBA who consults and conducts research in PM settings. Dr. H. was hired by a medical computer data-entry service to increase productivity. Workers at this company sat at desks wearing headphones and they typed patient records that had been voice-recorded by physicians. To get more work done faster (and thus more money for the data-entry company), Dr. H. recommended that data entry clerks increase their productivity by twenty percent. This would mean that breaks needed to be shorter or typing needed to be faster. Dr. H. wanted to pay incentives to staff members for each additional record that was typed beyond some specified quota.

The benefit was that workers might be able to make more money. Were there any risks that Dr. H. should have worried about?

(c) Because behavior analysts' scientific and professional judgments and actions affect the lives of others, they are alert to and guard against personal, financial, social, organizational, or political factors that might lead to misuse of their influence.

Researchers have a somewhat elevated status in our culture and are often looked to for advice or recommendations; that being the case, they need to be careful not to let their opinions be influenced by factors unrelated to the scientific data that is available.

CASE EXAMPLE AND QUESTION 79: DR. X.

Dr. X. was a very well-known behavior analyst and researcher. He had been published in many journals and was a well-recognized speaker at conferences and seminars. Dr. X. was offered a high-

powered, high-paying job by a private company in another state that offered comprehensive services to people with DD. The company had a residential facility, sheltered workshops, and a private school. Dr. X. could not resist going to work for this company as the new director of research. Once he was settled in his new job, Dr. X. realized that the private company was not so much interested in a sound behavior program and behavioral research as it was using his name and reputation to justify what they wanted to do. In some areas, the company wanted to jump on the bandwagon of popular trends that had not been substantiated by research.

Dr. X. has to make some choices. What can he do?

(d) Behavior analysts do not participate in activities in which it appears likely that their skills or data will be misused by others, unless corrective mechanisms, i.e., peer or external professional or independent review, are available.

Behavior analyst researchers must be wary of forums where their experimental work can be used to support a cause or organization that is not supported by the data.

CASE EXAMPLE AND QUESTION 80:
DR. ROGER A.

Dr. Roger A. was a BCBA who had an excellent reputation. He consulted in a number of DD agencies and he was on the faculty at a university. Dr. A. believed in community service, so he served on the local Human Rights Committee and he was on the board of directors of a local parents group (for parents of DD and autistic children). Dr. A. had published research on teaching social skills to children with developmental disabilities. Some of the more vocal parent activists found out about Dr. A.'s research. Using Dr.

A.'s socialization studies as their ammunition, they went to the school their children attended and caused a ruckus, demanding that their children be placed in regular education classrooms. Dr. A. was mortified that this happened. The worst part of this fiasco was that his studies had nothing to do with DD or autistic children being placed in regular classes.

What should Dr. A. do?

(e) Behavior analysts do not exaggerate claims for effectiveness of particular procedures or of behavior analysis in general.

It is important for the credibility of our field that behavior analysts "stick to the data" when explaining their results to others. In particular, it is important that the ethical behavior analyst in no way exaggerate the success of his or her procedures or of behavior analysis more generally, to do so lessens the credibility of the field.

CASE EXAMPLE AND QUESTION 81A:
DR. VIRGINIA G.

Dr. Virginia G. was a researcher who worked with autistic children. Dr. G. conducted one study with two preschool children with autism. In her study, Dr. G. arranged for the children to attend a preschool class with children who had no disabilities. Dr. G. arranged for the children to have a 1:1 behavior specialist and an additional aide throughout the day. The results of the research showed that the children with autism acquired many new skills while in the class and their behavior problems were easily managed. Dr. G. was thrilled. She wrote up the results of the research, making the bold statement that autistic children do not need special education classes and they can all be treated in the context of classes with typical children.

Dr. G. had the data which showed that her participants did great. Is there any problem with her conclusions?

(f) If behavior analysts learn of misuse or misrepresentation of their individual work products, they take reasonable and feasible steps to correct or minimize the misuse or misrepresentation.

Some important studies in behavior analysis get picked up by the media or advocates, and in an effort to build support, the actual results may be distorted. If this should happen to something that you have published, you have an obligation to try and correct the record.

CASE EXAMPLE AND QUESTION 81B:
DR. VIRGINIA G.

In Case 81a, when the research was completed, Dr. G. had the university's public relations director send press releases about the findings of her study to several magazines. (Although Dr. G. planned on sending the study to a scientific journal, she wanted the results sent to popular press magazines as well.) Dr. G. found out that the public relations director had put the following spin on the press releases: "Dramatic New Advances in Autism: Autistic Children Don't Need Special Education."

What should Dr. G. do?

USING CONFIDENTIAL INFORMATION FOR DIDACTIC OR INSTRUCTIVE PURPOSES (7.02)

(a) Behavior analysts do not disclose in their writings, lectures, or other public media, confidential, personally identifiable information concerning their individual or organizational clients, students, research participants, or other recipients of their services that they obtained during the course of

their work, unless the person or organization has consented in writing or unless there is other ethical or legal authorization for doing so.

Behavior analysts must always go out of their way to protect the identity of their experimental participants in their publications or presentations. It is wise to seek consent, in writing, if you foresee needing to do otherwise. In some rare instances, you may be required by the legal system to reveal confidential information.

CASE EXAMPLE AND QUESTION 82:
DR. RICHARD J. AND COURTNEY

Dr. Richard J. was a CBA who worked in a mental health facility. Dr. J. had known one of the office assistants, Courtney, since she was fifteen years old. Dr. J. met Courtney when she was a participant in research he conducted at a drug treatment facility. Now Courtney was twenty-two years old and she had been "clean" since she was nineteen. She was working part time in the mental health facility's office and she was attending community college classes. It finally looked like she had her life under control. Dr. J. was extremely impressed with Courtney's success. On several occasions, Dr. J. told staff members about Courtney's background and how she should be an inspiration to others. Dr. J. also talked about Courtney as a success case when he gave presentations at conferences. Dr. J. knew about issues pertaining to confidentiality, but he thought Courtney could be an inspiration to his colleagues at the facility and professionals at conferences who needed to hear an example of someone whose life was changed as a result of behavioral treatment.

The colleagues to whom Dr. J. spoke to about Courtney were professionals in the field and he knew they would not talk about her with other people. Considering this, was it acceptable for Dr. J. to tell other people about Courtney?

(b) Ordinarily, in such scientific and professional presentations, behavior analysts disguise confidential information concerning such persons or organizations so that they are not individually identifiable to others and so that discussions do not cause harm to participants who might identify themselves.

If you are publishing information or giving talks about your participants, it is a good idea to use made-up names and other masked references to avoid causing any harm to those who might associate themselves with your study.

CASE EXAMPLE AND QUESTION 83:
DR. GEORGE S. AND BILLY

Dr. George S. was a BCBA who was a university professor. He gave lectures to psychology and special education students and he frequently gave presentations and seminars at conferences. In his personal life, Dr. S. and his wife decided to become foster parents to a seven-year-old, Billy. Billy had been neglected by his substance-abusing mother when he was an infant. At four years of age, after an incident of sexual abuse (and a suspicion of many more incidents), Billy was removed from the home of his biological parents. From the time he was four until he was seven years old, Billy was in and out of foster homes. He was a very attractive child but he had severe behavior problems. When he was seven, Billy went to live with Dr. S. and his wife. Over the next two years, Billy had a loving home and a very intensive behavior analysis program. His behavior got much better and Dr. S. and his wife adopted Billy. Dr. S. had never been so proud of anything in his life as he was about Billy. Dr. S. frequently talked about Billy in his classes and at conferences, telling Billy's whole background, including the sexual abuse, information on his diagnoses, and his family history. At the end of one session, someone came up to Dr. S. and said, "You have done a great job with Billy and I know you are well intended, but aren't you violating Billy's right to confidentiality?"

> *Dr. S. said that Billy was his child and as the parent, he had the authority to disclose the information. Do you think this is correct?*

CONFORMING WITH LAWS AND REGULATIONS (7.03)

Behavior analysts plan and conduct research in a manner consistent with federal and state law and regulations, as well as professional standards governing the conduct of research, and particularly those standards governing research with human participants and animal subjects.

Behavior analysts involved in research need to be aware that some federal and state laws may regulate the manner in which human and animal subjects may be involved.

INFORMED CONSENT (7.04)

(a) Using language that is reasonably understandable to participants, behavior analysts inform participants of the nature of the research; they inform participants that they are free to participate or to decline to participate or to withdraw from the research; they explain the foreseeable consequences of declining or withdrawing; they inform participants of significant factors that may be expected to influence their willingness to participate (such as risks, discomfort, adverse effects, or limitations on confidentiality, except as provided in Standard 7.05 below); and they explain other aspects about which the prospective participants inquire.

(b) For persons who are legally incapable of giving informed consent, behavior analysts nevertheless (1) provide an appropriate explanation, (2) discontinue research if the person gives clear signs of unwillingness to continue participation, and (3) obtain appropriate permission from a legally authorized person, if such substitute consent is permitted by law.

Behavior analysts, with the intention of protecting their participants from any distress or duress, should inform them that their participation is completely voluntary and that they can drop out at any time. Further, the participants should be informed in writing about any aspects of the study that present any risk of harm and behavior analysts should answer completely any questions that potential participants might ask.

A significant amount of behavioral research is done with persons who are not really capable of giving consent. In these cases, the ethical behavior analyst will always obtain permission from the legal representative of the individual; further, the behavior analyst should build into his or her protocol some contingency plan for determining if the individual, although not capable of giving consent, nonetheless shows signs of distress and a desire to drop out.

CASE EXAMPLE AND QUESTION 84:
KAREN AND WANDA

Karen was a CBA who was a doctoral student. She was beginning some research in group homes for adult, ambulatory, verbal clients with developmental disabilities. Karen went to the group homes after the clients got back from the sheltered workshop and she observed their leisure skills. Karen decided to do her study in one house with four young women. She wanted to focus on arts and crafts and she purchased a large number of attractive new materials from her local craft store. Several weeks into the intervention (which involved having materials available, prompting usage, and providing social praise), one client, Wanda, decided she no longer wanted to work on crafts. Wanda wanted to spend her time outside shooting baskets. This was a disaster for Karen because her major professor had told her she could have no less than four participants in her study. Karen observed for a few days to make sure Wanda's interest in basketball was not a novelty. Unfortunately, the rainy summer weather had stopped and athletic Wanda was ready to be outside every day.

Would it be unethical for Karen to add some additional high-powered reinforcers just for Wanda?

DECEPTION IN RESEARCH (7.05)

(a) Behavior analysts do not conduct a study involving deception unless they have determined that the use of deceptive techniques is justified by the study's prospective scientific, educational, or applied value and that equally effective alternative procedures that do not use deception are not feasible.

Ordinarily, behavior analysts are not involved in research involving deception, and the requirement that research participants must give informed consent further decreases this form of dishonest conduct. Only in rare cases might some form of pretext be acceptable (e.g., where exact knowledge of a target behavior or type of intervention might affect the behavior adversely).

CASE EXAMPLE AND QUESTION 85: FRANK

Frank was a CBA who was a doctoral student. Frank was preparing to conduct research in a PM setting. He was going to work with warehouse workers on safety behaviors. The warehouse had two levels and workers frequently had to climb ladders and place boxes on the second level. Management was concerned because very frequently, the workers did not correctly set the "safety feet" on the ladders. There had been two falls, and when someone falls to concrete from a ladder, the injuries can be severe. So that Frank could get a baseline that was not affected by his observations, he trained the workers on proper lifting procedures. This had nothing to do with Frank's study, and it gave the workers the impression they were being observed for lifting techniques.

The Guidelines state that behavior analysts will not be involved in re-search involving deception. Was Frank in violation of the Guidelines?

(b) Behavior analysts never deceive research participants about significant aspects that would affect their willingness to participate, such as physical risks, discomfort, or unpleasant emotional experiences.

It is a given that behavior analysts would never trick individuals into participating if there was any chance that doing so might increase risk of physical harm or adversely affect their emotional state.

CASE EXAMPLE AND QUESTION 86: CARLOS

Carlos was a CBA who worked on a dual-diagnosis (mental health and mental retardation) unit of a state hospital. He was doing a research project with two men who were very physically aggressive, particularly toward women. Carlos wanted to determine if there would be less aggression if women talked to the aggressive men using a firm voice and instructions (rather than showing any signs of being docile). Carlos asked several female staff members from around the facility if they would be willing to participate in his study. He did not specifically tell them that in some of the sessions, he would ask them to approach the men in a docile, timid manner (and that he believed this might result in aggression).

If Carlos was correct and the study had clear findings, there would be implications for teaching women to interact with these clients in a way that would prevent the aggression. Considering this, was it ethical for Carlos to proceed as planned?

(c) Any other deception that is an integral feature of the design and conduct of an experiment must be explained to participants as early as is feasible,

preferably at the conclusion of their participation, but no later than at the conclusion of the research.

If the researcher used a "cover story" to disguise some aspect of his or her study, the participants should be told about this as soon as their participation is completed and not later than the end of the research (i.e., they receive a debriefing and have an opportunity to ask questions).

CASE EXAMPLE AND QUESTION 87: DR. M.

Dr. M. was advising a student at the end of the spring semester about what courses to take in the fall. In the course of the conversation, the student began talking about a "dating study" that she participated in and how disappointed she was that she did not find an "ideal mate" as she had been promised. When Dr. M. inquired if she had been debriefed at the end of the study, she said "no" and further, that the graduate student who ran the study did not answer phone messages or e-mails that she sent.

Dr. M. knew about the study and that it did not involve dating at all, but was rather a study on racial stereotyping. As a behavior analyst, what are his obligations?

INFORMING OF FUTURE USE (7.06)

Behavior analysts inform research participants of their anticipated sharing or further use of personally identifiable research data and of the possibility of unanticipated future uses.

Participants should be told that you plan to share your data with others (e.g., conference presentations, publication). Note that the sharing of "identifiable research data" is problematic with certain kinds of data, given the recent Health Insurance Portability and Accountability Act of 1996 (HIPAA). You should tell clients that you may continue to present the research at future conferences and that you will not reveal any identifying information such as their name, where they live, and so forth.

MINIMIZING INTERFERENCE (7.07)

In conducting research, behavior analysts interfere with the participants or environment from which data are collected only in a manner that is warranted by an appropriate research design and that is consistent with behavior analysts' roles as scientific investigators.

Because a great deal of applied behavioral research is carried out in the participants' own setting, the behavior analyst must do everything possible to avoid intrusion or disturbance. Further, it is important for behavior analysts to stick to their research protocol and not attempt to collect any data beyond that agreed to initially by the participants and as approved by the IRB.

CASE EXAMPLE AND QUESTION 88: HOWARD S.

Howard S. was a graduate student who was going to conduct some behavioral research in a nursing home. He had reviewed the literature in the area of behavioral geriatrics and he wanted to work on ambulation programs for older people. This was an important area of study because people in nursing homes often refuse to walk or exercise. Howard read about one study that was done on the research unit of a geriatric hospital. In this research facility, when the researchers studied increasing walking distances, they had participants walk in the long halls of the nursing home unit. They marked the walls with tape to indicate how far participants had walked. When the clients were settled back in their rooms, the researchers went with a measuring tape, measured the distance, and removed the small pieces of masking tape from the walls. After getting his research approved, Howard came up with a different idea about the way to measure distance walked. He decided that he would leave the tape on the walls and write the dates on each piece of tape so that clients could see their progress from one day to the next. The nursing home administrator did not like this idea. She told Howard that the facility was committed to making the nursing home an attractive, home-like environment and pieces of tape from multiple clients every day was not a good idea. This seemed like a small issue but it caused a major problem between Howard and the administrator. Red-faced and raging, Howard told his major professor that the administrator was an idiot and she did not understand the importance of research.

What do the Guidelines say that would give Howard some direction regarding the tape on the walls?

COMMITMENTS TO RESEARCH PARTICIPANTS (7.08)

Behavior analysts take reasonable measures to honor all commitments they have made to research participants.

If you make a promise to your participants (e.g., you have told them they will receive a fee or some service for participating), it is important that you follow through.

ENSURING PARTICIPANT ANONYMITY (7.09)

In presenting research, the behavior analyst ensures participant anonymity unless specifically waived by the participant or surrogate.

Behavior analysts should guarantee research participants that their names will not be divulged in print or in any future oral presentation; note that if they should waive this offer of anonymity, it is acceptable. However, the common protocol for research is that no names are used. Researchers are studying phenomena, not individuals, so names are not really relevant.

INFORMING OF WITHDRAWAL (7.10)

The behavior analyst informs the participant that withdrawal from the research may occur at any time without penalty except as stipulated in advance, as in fees contingent upon completing a project.

As a behavior analyst researcher you should, at the outset of the study, inform your participants that they may withdraw at any time without adverse consequences (unless, of course, there was some agreed on contingency at the beginning).

DEBRIEFING (7.11)

The behavior analyst informs the participant that debriefing will occur on conclusion of the participant's involvement in the research

Also, at the outset of the study, you should inform your research participants that they would have a debriefing at the end of the study.

ANSWERING RESEARCH QUESTIONS (7.12)

The behavior analyst answers all questions of the participant about the research that are consistent with being able to conduct the research.

During the debriefing, the behavior analyst answers all questions pertaining to the study.

WRITTEN CONSENT (7.13)

The behavior analyst must obtain the written consent of the participant or surrogate before beginning the research.

Before your research can begin, you must obtain written consent (a form that you prepare in advance that is signed) from each participant or his or her legal representative.

EXTRA CREDIT (7.14)

If the behavior analyst recruits participants from classes and the partici-
pants are provided additional credit for participating in the research, non-
participating students must be provided alternative activities that generate
comparable credit.

Behavior analysts who are doing research with students (e.g., college instruction) often offer extra credit for participating; if you do
this, you must also offer some way for nonparticipating students to
earn similar credits (i.e., they may not be disadvantaged in their grade
for the course by not being selected as a research participant).

CASE EXAMPLE AND QUESTION 89: DR. ABDUL Z.

Dr. Abdul Z. was teaching a behavior analysis class to under-
graduate students. Dr. Z. was a researcher and he told students if
they wanted to be data collection observers on one of his research
projects, they could earn extra credit for the class. The extra
points were added to class points and the course was graded on a
curve (based on who had the highest number of points). Some of
the students who were unavailable to take data felt that this sys-
tem was very unfair. They complained to Dr. Z. who said that he
believed in using behavior analysis principles and students who
showed more initiative should be rewarded.

What do the Guidelines say about this?

ACKNOWLEDGING CONTRIBUTIONS (7.15)

In presenting research, the behavior analyst acknowledges the contribu-
tions of others who contributed to the conduct of the research by including
them as co-authors or footnoting their contributions.

Behavior analysts who present or publish their work should recognize those who made an important contribution by including

them as coauthors or giving them a footnote. Coauthorship is for members of the research team who contributed a substantial amount to the research (e.g., Could you have done it without them? Did they have input into the goals and design of the study? Did they have input regarding methodology?) Footnotes are appropriate for data collectors, research assistants who looked up articles, and so forth.

CASE EXAMPLE AND QUESTION 90: LAURA

Laura was a graduate student who completed a master's thesis in a middle school. In the course of conducting her study on classroom behavior, Laura worked with several teachers, teacher aides, and the school guidance counselor on a regular basis. The teachers and aides took data and the guidance counselor met with Laura four times to provide academic background information on the children. Laura met at least one time per week with her major professor. He guided her as she planned the study and data collection systems. In addition, one night per week, Laura attended a research meeting for graduate students. Each week, she reported on her progress and the students asked questions and made suggestions for the study. When the study was completed, written, and ready to submit to a journal, Laura had a hard time deciding who should be listed as authors and the order in which names should be listed. She listed herself first, then her major professor, then the teachers in alphabetical order, the aides in alphabetical order, the guidance counselor, and two students from the research meeting. There were ten authors listed on the manuscript. Laura's major professor told her some of the people listed needed to be credited in a footnote.

Who should be moved to the footnote?

PRINCIPAL AUTHORSHIP AND OTHER PUBLICATION CREDITS (7.16)

Principal authorship and other publication credits accurately reflect the relative scientific or professional contributions of the individuals involved, regardless of their relative status. Mere possession of an institutional position, such as Department Chair, does not justify authorship credit. Minor contributions to the research or to the writing for publications are appropriately acknowledged, such as in footnotes or in an introductory statement. Further, these Guidelines recognize and support the ethical requirements for authorship and publication practices contained in the ethical code of the American Psychological Association.

Behavior analysts involved in research will need to determine, at the time an article is submitted for review, those names that will be included, and what the order will be if several people made important contributions. The general rule is that the person who made the most significant contribution goes in the first position ("first author") and that other names after that reflect lesser degrees of contribution ("co-authors") in rank order. First authors should resist the temptation to include the name of anyone who simply made some small contribution to the research. Those who did help in lesser ways should be acknowledged in a footnote or possibly a statement at the top of the article.

CASE EXAMPLE AND QUESTION 91

A large mental health agency provided comprehensive community services that included staff training, behavioral consultation for clients, and consultation on the mental health unit at the local hospital. Periodically, behavioral researchers from the university became involved in agency projects and applied research would be conducted. On more than one project, everything went well until it came time to submit an article based on the research. The faculty member who designed the research and wrote the first draft of the manuscript wanted himself listed as the first author and generously, in his mind, listed everyone else in a footnote. Students who served as data collectors were angry when they found out they would not be listed as coauthors; they had heard from graduate students that getting your name on a publication was a "ticket to grad school" and now felt like they had no chance of getting in after having spent six-months on this project.

Looking back, how should this have been handled differently?

PAYING PARTICIPANTS (7.17)

The behavior analyst who pays participants for research involvement or uses money as a reinforcer must obtain Institutional Review Board or Human Rights Committee approval of this practice and conform to any special requirements that may be established in the process of approval.

The use of money as a reinforcer for research participation can present special problems; if you are using money you must make sure this is specified in your application to the IRB or HRC (Human Rights Committee).

CASE EXAMPLE AND QUESTION 92: BEVERLY

Beverly, a CBA, was a doctoral student who worked with low-income parents and their children. Beverly was beginning the research for her doctoral dissertation and she decided to work with families who lived in a neighboring county (twenty-five miles away) to prevent working with any clients with whom she had consulted. Beverly's study involved having the parents bring their children to the university speech lab, and teaching the parents how to use behavioral procedures to teach new language skills.

Beverly's research had been approved by her committee, the agency who referred the parents, and by the IRB. Beverly had approval from the IRB to pay the parents a flat fee for gas reimbursement. After the third session with one family, the mother made a comment to Beverly about how gas prices were going up and coming to these sessions was expensive. Beverly was afraid this family might drop out of the study. She decided to give these parents an incentive for coming to the sessions. She told the mother she would add $5 to the gas money for each session the family attended, plus, she said, "I'll also throw in $20 so you can take the kids to get hamburgers on the way home."

Are there any circumstances under which these additional incentives would have been acceptable?

WITHHOLDING PAYMENT (7.18)

The behavior analyst who withholds part of the money earned by the participant until the participant has completed their research involvement must inform the participant of this condition prior to beginning the experiment.

If you are using money as a reinforcer and have some contingency that says the participants only receive it if they complete the whole experiment, you must tell them this at the outset of the study.

GRANT REVIEWS (7.19)

The behavior analyst who serves on grant review panels avoids conducting any research described in grant proposals that the behavior analyst reviewed, except as replications fully crediting the prior researchers.

Some professional behavior analyst researchers may be invited by granting agencies to serve on peer-review committees to evaluate research proposals. This gives them access to research ideas from other investigators that are still in the early stages of development. It is considered unethical for those behavior analysts who serve on such committees to use those ideas in their own research (except in the case of replications, and here they must give credit to the earlier researchers).

CASE EXAMPLE AND QUESTION 93: DR. DANIEL V.

Dr. Daniel V. was a behavioral researcher at a university. His specialties were learning disabilities and teaching reading. He also taught graduate seminars. Dr. V. was asked to serve on a grant review committee. In his role on the grant review committee, Dr. V. went to Washington, DC twice a year. He and other researchers would convene at a large conference table for three days and review grant submissions. In one meeting, several grant proposals had been submitted that addressed the teaching of reading to children with learning disabilities. Dr. V. was amazed to see in this proposal some new strategies for assessing reading skills and teaching reading. He recommended that the grant be funded. As soon as Dr. V. got back to his own lab at the university, he quickly began some pilot research on the same topic, using the procedures he had read in the grant proposal. He felt that the results would be published anyway and by the time his research was done, the other researchers would probably be credited in the literature.

Was Dr. V. correct?

ANIMAL RESEARCH (7.20)

Behavior analysts who conduct research involving animals treat them humanely and are in compliance with the Federal Animal Welfare Act.

Behavior analyst who are involved in animal research treat them with compassion and comply with the U.S. Code, Title 7, Ch. 54, of the Federal Animal Welfare Act and Regulations (1990).

RESPONSES TO CASE QUESTION 72A: RON

The coach's permission was not enough for Ron to do this research. He should have followed the protocol for all research that is done with human participants. Ron needed to submit a detailed proposal to the IRB and any other relevant local human research committees. His major professor should have known he was conducting research on another part of campus. Further, developing the intervention strategy as he "went along" was not in accordance with the Guidelines. The interventions needed to be detailed in the written research proposal and justified based on previous published research.

RESPONSES TO CASE QUESTION 72B: RON

According to the Guidelines, the results of research need to be presented in the most truthful, accurate manner possible. Behavior analysts should not present data so that the results are misleading. It was not appropriate to pick and choose the best participants for data presentation. Ron does not appear ready to do applied research and seems not to have a good understanding of the fundamental ethics and procedures involved. He needs both an ethics seminar and a graduate research methods class.

RESPONSES TO CASE QUESTION 73

The Guidelines state that behavior analysts who are doing research will look after the safety and well-being of the participants. In the street-crossing study, observers simply took data during baseline. However, observers were very well-trained and they understood that nothing was more important than the safety of the children. Observers were placed at critical locations nearby and they were prepared to intervene immediately if it appeared that a child was in harm's way.

RESPONSES TO CASE QUESTION 74: DR. YUNG-HA C. AND KIRSTEN

Dr. C. should be reminded that he is responsible for the ethical conduct of research of anyone on his research team. He needs to pay a visit to the school and work with Kirsten. If she cannot be counted on to follow the protocol or be a reliable observer, she needs to be removed from the research project.

RESPONSES TO CASE QUESTION 75: CARL

Carl needed an approval of the IRB before starting any research in the schools. The approval from school personnel was not sufficient.

RESPONSES TO CASE QUESTION 76: SHONDRA

Shondra needs to notify her advisor and her committee. Few beginning researchers realize this, but she should also notify the IRB that the circumstances have changed and that a modified proposal may be forthcoming. The IRB is available to give advice and assistance throughout the course of a research project. It is not merely a body that gives a one time approval at the beginning of a study.

RESPONSES TO CASE QUESTION 77: BRUCE

As a behavior analyst who was doing research in the context of behavioral programming, Bruce would be expected to do research that follows a behavior analytic model. He could choose to use music as an intervention, and take data using standard data collection systems and single subject design. Rather than ask clients how music "made them feel," Bruce could evaluate if music resulted in decreases in specified maladaptive target behaviors or increased prosocial behaviors.

RESPONSES TO CASE QUESTION 78: DR. SAM H.

When you are pushing people to do more physically, you need to make sure that any negative effects are outweighed by the benefits of the study. In the case of Dr. H., he would want to make sure that staff members take adequate breaks. It is hard to sit and type all day long and an intervention that decreased break times (where people can stretch muscles by moving around) could result in neck and back problems, carpal tunnel syndrome, and so forth.

RESPONSES TO CASE QUESTION 79: DR. X.

Dr. X. can hope his old job is still open, he can look for a new job, or he can work to convince the company owners or board, and so forth, that they need to have a reputable behavior analysis program. He could bring in outside experts to meet with them and he could begin getting appropriate recognition for the program by doing behavior analytic research.

RESPONSES TO CASE QUESTION 80: DR. ROGER A.

The Guidelines caution behavior analysts about being a part of forums where their research can be used to support a cause that is not supported by the data. If the parents were generally reasonable and this appeared to be a one-time problem, Dr. A. could calm the waters by contacting the school, explaining that he had no part in this, and educating the parents about why this was a mistake. However, if after some careful thought, Dr. A. decided that he was in the midst of some radical, hard-to-manage parents, he may be better off to resign from the Board. This is a difficult stance to take, but the behavior analyst should not allow another person or group to damage his or her professional reputation.

RESPONSES TO CASE QUESTION 81A: DR. VIRGINIA G.

Simply put, Dr. G. overstated her case. She only worked with two children and she cannot generalize to the whole population based on this. She needs to present her data clearly and explain that for some children, her treatment may not have worked. The Guidelines warn behavior analysts about exaggerating the effectiveness of their procedures.

RESPONSES TO CASE QUESTION 81B: DR. VIRGINIA G.

Dr. G. needs to "stop the presses" on the press releases. Behavior analysts should correct any misrepresentation of their work. This study dealt with only two children, there was a tremendous support system in place such that the children weren't really functioning independently in regular education, and such a claim would be false.

RESPONSES TO CASE QUESTION 82:
DR. RICHARD J. AND COURTNEY.

Dr. J. should not have given identifying information about Courtney or talked about her past with his colleagues or conference participants. Behavior analysts do not disclose in their writings personally identifiable information about clients or research participants. By telling his colleagues about Courtney, it could affect the way that people relate to her or interact with her. If Courtney chooses to tell her own story, that is her privilege, which is protected by the First Amendment.

RESPONSES TO CASE QUESTION 83:
DR. GEORGE S. AND BILLY

At some point, Billy was a foster child and Dr. S. was talking about those experiences and using Billy's name. According to the Guidelines, behavior analysts should disguise confidential information (i.e., Billy's diagnoses, his family history) and the person's identity. Billy has been adopted by Dr. S., so he will be around for years. It might embarrass Billy to have everyone who meets him knowing about his past. Dr. S. could talk about procedures and how his child reacted to them, such as, "When I used intensive toilet training with my son, he resisted the overcorrection." This is a good place for behavior analysts to think of how they would like to be treated. Not many people would want others to know that they had been sexually abused, and so forth.

RESPONSES TO CASE QUESTION 84: KAREN AND WANDA

Karen should have had a contingency plan so that participants could make the choice to drop out. She should also have had extra participants so if someone dropped out, it would not affect her study. A researcher should not want a participant involved in the study for the wrong reasons, such as when the participant is there only to get the reinforcers rather than because the participant enjoys the activity. To ensure that participants don't drop out, procedures should be used such as careful screening and participant selection in the beginning, reinforcer sampling, and so forth. A good reinforcer sampling assessment might have shown Karen that Wanda did not especially like indoor activities that involved sitting and fine motor skills.

RESPONSES TO CASE QUESTION 85: FRANK

This case could go either way. If Frank told the workers he was specifically looking at lifting techniques, but he was actually observing behaviors related to safety on the ladders, he deceived the participants. He should have told the workers he would be looking at a variety of safety behaviors. He could do the training on proper lifting to help the company and if the workers came to the conclusion he was observing lifting, this was their own assumption.

Behavior analysts don't usually get involved in research that is specifically designed to study deception, as in, "How would college students react in a study when they have been lied to?"

Another example of an unethical, deceptive practice in research would be to tell a teacher you were observing child behavior when you were actually taking data on teacher behavior. At a minimum, the teacher should be told you are observing teacher–child interactions.

RESPONSES TO CASE QUESTION 86: CARLOS

Participants should always be informed of any chance of physical harm or discomfort. In this case, if Carlos suspected one way of interacting with the

*clients prevented aggression, he could have looked at data under those con-
ditions. He should not, however, have a condition where he specifically in-
structs research participants to behave in a way that he knows will result in
the clients becoming physically aggressive toward the women. In the rare
cases where aggression is prompted so it can be treated, this is done by a
therapy team (not by research participants).*

RESPONSES TO CASE QUESTION 87: DR. M.

*Dr. M. is in a delicate spot because this student is clearly upset and he knows
that she was mislead about her participation in an experiment conducted
by a colleague of his in the psychology department. Because that faculty
member is not a behavior analyst, this code does not necessarily apply to
him, but Dr. M. knows that a comparable code item in the APA code of ethics does apply (Standards 6.15 and 6.18). Dr. M. is obligated to bring this to
the attention of his faculty colleague.*

RESPONSES TO CASE QUESTION 88: HOWARD S.

*The Guidelines say that behavior analysts do everything possible to avoid
intrusion or disturbance. Howard was being intrusive in this facility, not
necessarily by requiring a lot of staff, but by trying to alter the environment
the administrator wished to maintain.*

RESPONSES TO CASE QUESTION 89: DR. ABDUL Z.

*According to the Guidelines, if some members of a class are given extra
credit, all class members must be given a chance to earn extra credit. Dr. Z.
should have provided some alternative extra credit assignments for students who were not observers on his project.*

RESPONSES TO CASE QUESTION 90: LAURA

*Laura should list herself first because she is the primary investigator. Her
major professor should be listed second, given the guidance that he provided*

on this particular research. In some cases, major professors choose to be listed last in all publications, other than those projects they conducted alone. This is a "signature" of the professor. Other professors will determine how much input they had relative to the student and other members of the research team and they may ask to be listed third or fourth. This might be the case if two students were basically coresearchers on a project and the professor provided guidance to them. If one or more of the teachers gave critical input for the study, such as designing data sheets or developing methodology, they should be listed as coauthors. Otherwise, everyone else is credited in a footnote.

RESPONSES TO CASE QUESTION 91

Authorship and publication credits reflect the relative contributions of the individuals involved. Researchers are listed as authors with the name of the primary person listed first. Data collectors, students who look up articles, and people who carry out some of the client interventions, are usually given a footnote acknowledgment. The American Psychological Association (APA) provides some guidelines for authorship in the APA manual under "publication practices." Basically, the faculty member or researcher who has clearly been down this road before should have specified in advance the type of credit that each person would receive if the research was successful and ultimately written up and submitted for publication.

RESPONSES TO CASE QUESTION 92: BEVERLY

If Beverly decided to change the incentives for the study, she needed to go back to the IRB and get approval for a gas reimbursement increase and approval for the meal money. It is not ethical for Beverly to pay one family more for gas and to provide a meal if she is not going to do this for everyone. The only way she could have done this differentially would be to pay based on miles door to door and by doing this, some families may get more money for gas.

RESPONSES TO CASE QUESTION 93: DR. DANIEL V.

What is legal and what is ethical are often two different things. It is unethical for Dr. V. to use the work that he saw in a confidential grant review committee. Dr. V. took the high road and decided not to use the research ideas belonging to the other research team until the work was published.

Chapter 11

The Behavior Analyst's Ethical Responsibility to the Field of Behavior Analysis (Guideline 8)

Behavior analysis, although growing rapidly as a profession (G. L. Shook, personal communication, May 30, 2004), is still a very small field when compared to other related areas such as social work or clinical psychology. For the most part, we are not yet on the radar screens of most Americans, and, based on our past experience, we know that unethical conduct by a small number of persons can reflect badly on our whole field. If we are to gain the trust of the public we must set a very high standard of moral and ethical conduct. To be an ethical behavior analyst means not only upholding these Guidelines for your protection and the protection of your clients, but also preserving and enhancing the reputation of behavior analysis in general. Guideline 8.0 makes it clear that each and every one of us should "support the values of the field." This no doubt includes the nine core ethical principles discussed in chapter 2 as well as those values inherent in a behavioral approach. In addition to honesty, fairness, taking responsibility, and promoting autonomy, behavior analysts also promote the value of objective, reliable data in determining treatment effectiveness, in the use of that data in decision making, and in focusing on individual behavior as our primary focus of study. Behavior analysts value novel assessments, effective nonintrusive interventions, and the production of socially significant changes in behavior that have worth to the individual and to society. We believe in optimizing each individual's worth, dignity, and independence and in developing the repertoires necessary to accomplish these goals. It is sometimes necessary to remind our colleagues of these basic values and this Guideline provides this occasion.

Additionally, Guideline 8.0 is a prompt to all behavior analysts to promote our methodology and findings to the public (Guideline 8.02), and to ourselves, occasionally review the Guidelines so we are well aware of the standards that have been set. A somewhat onerous task involves monitoring other professionals (or paraprofessionals) in our community to make sure that they do not misrepresent themselves as certified when they are not. This vigilance is warranted by considering the harm that could be done to clients by practitioners who are not properly trained. The additional harm to the reputation of our field should something happen to a client is also a constant worry to those who work hard to maintain high standards. It is basically unethical to turn a blind eye to those who are misrepresenting themselves as BCBAs® when they are not. How one "discourages" these noncertified individuals is not spelled out in the Guidelines, but presumably contacting the BACB would be a first step; another might involve contacting ABA or your local state association for advice and assistance.

THE BEHAVIOR ANALYST'S ETHICAL RESPONSIBILITY TO THE FIELD OF BEHAVIOR ANALYSIS (8.0)

The behavior analyst has a responsibility to support the values of the field, to disseminate knowledge to the public, to be familiar with these guidelines, and to discourage misrepresentation by non-certified individuals.

AFFIRMING PRINCIPLES (8.01)

The behavior analyst upholds and advances the values, ethics, principles, and mission of the field of behavior analysis; participation in both state and national or international behavior analysis organizations is strongly encouraged.

Behavior analysts have an obligation to speak out on behalf of the field and to support the values of the field. These include honesty, integrity, fairness, and the continuing search for basic principles of behavior that can be used to improve the human condition. To this end, the ethical behavior analyst attends and participates in the various organizations at the state, national, and international level.

CASE EXAMPLE AND QUESTION 94:
DR. CHRISTOPHER S.

Dr. Christopher S. is a CBA who has worked in DD settings for ten years. Dr. S. attends local chapter meetings to earn the minimum number of CEU credits required. Dr. S. has never traveled to a state association meeting or to the national Association for Behavior Analysis conference held in a different city in May of each year. Dr. S. does not have a family and he has plenty of money to travel. He has been described by some of his colleagues as "lazy" and by others as "indifferent" with regard to staying current with the field.

Does this rise to the level of unethical conduct?

DISSEMINATING BEHAVIOR ANALYSIS (8.02)

The behavior analyst assists the profession in making behavior analysis methodology available to the general public.

One area of responsibility to the field of behavior analysis involves helping to educate the general public about our profession. This might involve speaking at local civic groups, writing letters to the editor of the local newspaper to correct some misinformation about behavior analysis or participating in training workshops for parents, teachers, or other professionals on some aspect of behavior analysis methodology.

CASE EXAMPLE AND QUESTION 95: DR. B.

Dr. B. is a BCBA who teaches university classes in behavior analysis and as a hobby, started training his dog. When he got involved in competitive dog training, he saw that many dog trainers were misusing the principles of operant conditioning. He would occasionally prompt these uninformed trainers about the proper use of operant conditioning and spoke often of his experiences in his behavior analysis classes. One day while reviewing the BACB Guidelines, he noticed that behavior analysts have a "responsibility to the field" to help "educate the general public about our profession." Subsequently Dr. B. collaborated with a colleague and produced a book for dog trainers called "How Dogs Learn." The book was based on basic principles of behavior analysis.

What are some other areas where a creative behavior analyst could take the message of behavior analysis to the general public?

BEING FAMILIAR WITH THESE GUIDELINES (8.03)

Behavior analysts have an obligation to be familiar with these Guidelines, other applicable ethics codes, and their application to behavior analysts' work. Lack of awareness or misunderstanding of a conduct standard is not itself a defense to a charge of unethical conduct.

These Guidelines are designed to assist behavior analysts in the conduct of their professional lives. It is imperative that we all are acquainted with them as well as other ethics codes, which may be relevant. Ignorance of the standards is no excuse should you be accused of unethical behavior.

CASE EXAMPLE AND QUESTION 96: DARLA AND KEN

Darla was a CABA who was working for a behavioral services company that owned a residential facility, a sheltered workshop, and some group homes. Darla was a hard worker. She was somewhat shy but was well liked by other employees. Darla's supervisor, Ken, was a happily married BCBA and although he did not behave inappropriately around Darla, he often encouraged other staff members who were his good friends to invite Darla on dates, to parties, or to lunch or dinner. He felt like she should have a more active social life. Darla soon picked up on this manipulation and decided to have a talk with Ken. She told him she needed to let him know he was making her feel uncomfortable and possibly violating the behavior analyst's Guidelines for Responsible Conduct Standard 1.08a. Ken took offense at his well-meaning gestures and advised Darla to "lighten up." He said the Guidelines pertained to professional issues, and could not be used to "tell me how to live my life."

Did Darla go too far in suggesting that Ken was engaging in unethical conduct?

DISCOURAGING MISREPRESENTATION BY NON-CERTIFIED INDIVIDUALS (8.04)

Behavior analysts discourage non-certified practitioners from misrepresenting that they are certified.

Should you run into someone who presents himself or herself as a CBA or CABA, you have an obligation to point out the Guidelines and dissuade that person from representing himself or herself as a certified behavior analyst.

CASE EXAMPLE AND QUESTION 97

*Two CABAs have accepted positions at a privately-owned resi-
dential school for children with autism. In the last six months, the
school fired the director of behavior analysis and the three CBAs
who were on staff in an attempt to balance the budget. Parents of
the children paid more than $50,000 per year to have their chil-
dren in the program. The well-trained CABAs were horrified to
find out that behavioral programming was no longer being provided at this school. Under new fiscally conservative management, the program drifted to become a very exclusive baby-sitting
service for autistic children. On all of the printed literature and
web pages describing the school, the advertising clearly offers "behavior analytic treatment" as one of the services.*

What should the two CABAs do? Taking on the school administra-
tion sounds like it could cause a lot of trouble and cost them their
jobs.

RESPONSES TO CASE QUESTION 94: DR. CHRISTOPHER S.

*Dr. S. has no excuse for not attending conferences for his continuing profes-
sional development. Conferences are an opportunity to network with colleagues, learn about the latest innovative research, the newest cutting-edge
behavioral treatment techniques, and become a part of the behavioral community. Conferences give you a chance to meet the leading experts in behavior analysis. You can improve your technical skills by learning about
graphing, data collection systems, and so forth. You might get ideas for how
you can provide new services or programs for your clients.*

RESPONSES TO CASE QUESTION 95: DR. B.

*Behavior analysts can help educate parents by speaking at a PTO meeting,
they can talk to people in the hospitality industry about PM, and they can*

use good behavioral procedures informally at their jobs. When the local newspaper runs a story that has behavioral implications, a behavior analyst could write a letter to the editor outlining a good behavioral solution.

RESPONSES TO CASE QUESTION 96: DARLA AND KEN

According to Guideline 8.03, Ken, as a BCBA, is responsible for familiarity with the Guidelines. If he was familiar with the Guidelines, he would know about Section 1.08 (a) that pertains to "exploitative" relationships with supervisees. Although he does not consider his well-meaning gestures to be unethical, Darla does. He needs to be sensitive to her needs and realize that some people are very sensitive to manipulation and view it as a form of exploitation.

Ken should also know about Section 1.07. This section addresses multiple relationships. If Ken has a supervisory relationship with staff who are his "good friends," he potentially has some multiple relationship or conflict of interest problems as well. Ken would be well advised to read through the BACB Guidelines carefully to see what else he is missing.

RESPONSES TO CASE QUESTION 97

Problem number one is that these two associates are not supervised by a CBA. Problem number two is that, from this description, the program has no integrity, and the CABAs should rethink their association with the organization. First, they should go to the management and point out their concerns and the ethical issues connected with them. Next, if they get no response, they should consider quitting and reporting the organization to the BAC Board and to ABA. And, depending on what their relationship is with the parents they may wish, on their way out, to share some of their concerns.

Chapter 12

The Behavior Analyst's Ethical Responsibility to Colleagues (Guideline 9)

Behavior analysts have, in their vast catalog of work to be done, a clear set of responsibilities to their colleagues. If you are a practitioner or therapist, you may be concerned about possible ethical violations of other behavior analysts. It should first be understood that attending to a situation like this does not make you a "busybody" or "snitch." Most of us have been culturally conditioned by parents and teachers to "mind your own business," and in your private life, this is a pretty good rule to follow. How others conduct their lives really is their own business, unless, of course, it affects your life in some way. This is basically the situation you confront when you believe that a behavioral colleague has violated the BACB® Guidelines for Responsible Conduct. It becomes your business by virtue of the fact that an unethical colleague can stain not only their reputation but yours as well. It is in this vein that Guideline 9.01 is written to encourage you, despite how uncomfortable it may make you feel, to bring the issue in question to the attention of the person and seek a resolution. Ideally, the individual will quickly see the error of his or her ways, apologize, and correct the situation with appropriate action. It is not your job to dictate the action but rather to serve as a "trusted colleague" for the person on behalf of the field and

182

possibly the client who may have been involved.[1] In this role you should seek an ethical solution to the problem and then fade from the picture as quickly as possible. This works most of the time. However, it might happen that the colleague stubbornly resists recognizing the problem or refuses to do anything about it. This will present you with a dilemma that the Guidelines do not cover. If this happens, you may want to check the "Disciplinary Standards, Procedures for Appeals" section of the BACB Web site (BACB, 2004) for further details on what to do next.

The remainder of Guideline 9.0 has to do with the responsibility that academics have to their colleagues and to the world of research and publication. Here the Guidelines require that behavior analysts report their data accurately and honestly (Guideline 9.02), that they not commit plagiarism (Guideline 9.03), and that they share data that have been referred to in publication form (Guideline 9.05). Although not made explicit here, it is commonly accepted that behavior analyst researchers will share not only data but also other information on how a study was conducted so that other researchers, for the good of all concerned, can replicate the findings.

THE BEHAVIOR ANALYST'S ETHICAL RESPONSIBILITY TO COLLEAGUES (9.0)

Behavior analysts have an obligation to bring attention to and resolve ethical violations by colleagues, to make sure their data are accurate and presented truthfully, and they share data with colleagues.

No good purpose can be served by behavior analysts becoming aware of ethical violations but doing nothing to correct them. With regard to colleagues, we have an obligation to make sure our data are precise and properly represent our findings. In the interest of the advancement of science and the replication of our experiments, behavior analysts share their data with colleagues.

---

[1]Note that this Guideline does not cover any acts that constitute actual illegal behavior; in this case, you would need to contact the proper authorities and let them handle the matter.

ETHICAL VIOLATIONS BY COLLEAGUES (9.01)

When behavior analysts believe that there may have been an ethical viola-
tion by another behavior analyst, they attempt to resolve the issue by bring-
ing it to the attention of that individual if an informal resolution appears
appropriate and the intervention does not violate any confidentiality rights
that may be involved.

There could be some circumstance under which you determine
that another behavior analyst has engaged in some unethical conduct. It is your duty to try and resolve the issue by bringing it to the attention of the individual if (a) you believe that the issue can be
handled unofficially, and (b) your action will not violate any client's
confidentially. One item not specifically addressed by the Guidelines
is what to do when a professional who is not a behavior analyst engages in unethical conduct. You can talk to the person about the Code
of Ethics to which you adhere. Many other professions have a Code of
Ethics and if you mention the term "unethical," the person will get the
message. If you cannot resolve the issue by talking to the person, you
may have to talk to his or her supervisor.

CASE EXAMPLE AND QUESTION 98: MIRANDA

Miranda had been working for a "medicaid-waiver" organiza-
tion for about six months when she suddenly quit with no expla-
nation. Within a few days, the rumor mill had it that she had
begun taking clients privately, including some that she met
through her previous job.

If you were her (previous) supervisor what would you do?

ACCURACY OF DATA (9.02)

Behavior analysts do not fabricate data or falsify results in their publica-
tions. If behavior analysts discover significant errors in their published

data, they take reasonable steps to correct such errors in a correction, retraction, erratum, or other appropriate publication means.

As a field that lives by its data, we are exceedingly concerned that published data are absolutely true and properly represent the findings of a study. Therefore, behavior analysts are diligent and scrupulous about checking and double-checking their data to make sure that they are correct before they are sent in for publication. Should some error take place in the publication process such that the final manuscripts contains an error, the behavior analyst will take the necessary steps to make sure that the mistake is corrected.

AUTHORSHIP AND FINDINGS (9.03)

Behavior analysts do not present portions or elements of another's work or data as their own, even if the other work or data source is cited occasionally, nor do they omit findings that might alter others' interpretations of their work or behavior analysis in general.

Plagiarism in any form is unacceptable, unethical conduct. This includes not only written text but data and concepts as well. Always give citations for your sources.

CASE EXAMPLE AND QUESTION 99: ROGER N.

Roger N. was a CBA who liked attending workshops. Roger wanted to get the required number of CEU's each year, but he also felt he could stay current with the field of behavior analysis by attending state and national level workshops. Roger attended the same workshop, given by the same presenter, on three different occasions. Roger was very surprised when the workshop leader began to show slides and data that Roger recognized as being the work of someone else. At the end of the workshop, Roger approached the presenter and said, "Some of the slides and graphs you showed today look like information I have seen somewhere else. Was some of your data from the research that Dr. (name) has done—he presents this in his workshops." The presenter looked annoyed and told Roger it would be very distracting to give citations and references all the way through a six-hr workshop. He said that certainly, if he published someone's work, he would give credit, but workshop information can be shared. The Guidelines clearly address ethical standards for publishing research.

Do the Guidelines cover this situation?

PUBLISHING DATA (9.04)

Behavior analysts do not publish, as original data, data that have been previously published. This does not preclude republishing data when they are accompanied by proper acknowledgment.

When writing up your research for publication, remember that the original data can only be published once. If you later refer to this data in a subsequent article, you are required to cite your original publication. Under some circumstances, a manuscript may be published in a second journal but an explanatory note from the editor or author usually accompanies this.

CASE EXAMPLE AND QUESTION 100: MARGUERITE

Marguerite, an undergraduate psychology student, was taking a behavior analysis course in which students had to find articles that illustrated specific uses of behavior analysis. Students read the articles they found and wrote a short paper on each article. The professor asked that students attach a copy of the article to the paper in the event there were any questions about methodology, or the professor thought the student didn't understand a particular concept. Marguerite found an article on a topic she found interesting. She wrote the paper and turned in the article. She was looking for a new article a few weeks later and the names of the authors of the first article caught her eye. The article was in a different journal, but the data and writing were identical. Marguerite brought a copy of the article to class and asked the professor if this was a common practice.

Do the Guidelines cover this situation?

WITHHOLDING DATA (9.05)

After research results are published, behavior analysts do not withhold the data on which their conclusions are based from other competent professionals who seek to verify the substantive claims through reanalysis and who intend to use such data only for that purpose, provided that the confidentiality of the participants can be protected and unless legal rights concerning proprietary data preclude their release.

It is an ethic of behavior analysts that we share our data with others to strengthen the findings through transparency and replication. Should another behavior analyst request to see your raw data, you are obligated to provide it to them for the purpose of reanalysis. It is assumed that should someone request your data, you will take the necessary steps to protect the confidentiality of the participants. The only exception to sharing of data is in the case of data that has been trademarked, patented, or is somehow otherwise exclusively held by a company.

CASE EXAMPLE AND QUESTION 101: GORDON

Gordon was a CBA who was beginning his doctoral research in a university behavior analysis program. Gordon began outlining his study and as a first step, he reviewed all of the literature. He found one published study that was of major interest to him. The researchers had done something very similar to what Gordon planned to do. Gordon believed it would save him a lot of time if he could use a participant assessment tool that the authors of this study reportedly used. Although it was referred to, the assessment was not published in the journal article. With the approval of his major professor, Gordon contacted the first author of the study to inquire about the assessment. Gordon received no response from the first author despite repeated phone and e-mail messages. Then his major professor began trying to contact the authors. He too received no response. Finally, Gordon tried calling again, and the first author of the study happened to answer the phone. He told Gordon that he did not wish to share any information that was not published in the article. He said he may want to do future research and the assessment was not available for Gordon's use.

Do the Guidelines say anything that can help Gordon make his case?

RESPONSES TO CASE QUESTION 98: MIRANDA

Miranda's previous supervisor called her into his office and asked her to please describe what happened. She indicated that she thought she could make a little more money working for herself and that she was not getting that much out of supervision anyway. He produced a copy of the contract that she signed initially indicating that she would stay in the position for at least two years and that if she left prematurely she would not compete with the organization for business. Miranda was shocked to learn that her action was a violation of the BACB code of ethics. She agreed to return to her previous position and said that she would explain to the clients that it was her fault and that she would straighten the situation out. She also asked for a copy of the contract that she had previously signed.

RESPONSES TO CASE QUESTION 99: ROGER N.

According to Section 9.3 of the Guidelines, "behavior analysts do not present portions or elements of another's work as their own." The ethical behav-

ior analyst will give credit to the author of any work that is used, whether or not it has been published. Remember that what is ethical and what is legal are sometimes two different things. Several years ago, Dr. B. wrote a book on research methods. The book was self-published and was used for years as the curriculum for university students. The book made its way into the hands of someone who recognized that the book was not copyrighted. The person took the material and the Table of Contents and published a nearly identical book with a major publisher. Dr. B.'s original work was not even listed as one of the references. This was clearly unethical.

RESPONSES TO CASE QUESTION 100: MARGUERITE

A researcher can publish data that has been previously published if the data is accompanied by a proper acknowledgment. The main issue here is that researchers should not send virtually the same graphs and text to different journals to get additional publications from the same material ("double dipping").

RESPONSES TO CASE QUESTION 101: GORDON

The Guidelines say that behavior analysts do not withhold data on which their conclusions are based. This would seem to apply to background material for a study. Ethical researchers will provide the necessary information so that others can easily replicate their work or so that others do not have to reinvent the wheel when trying to start a very similar research project.

Chapter 13

The Behavior Analyst's Ethical Responsibility to Society (Guideline 10)

Behavior analysts, like all good citizens, are interested in promoting the general welfare of our society. With our expertise in analyzing contingencies of reinforcement, we have a particular interest in encouraging the culture to make better use of the knowledge we have gained over the past sixty years about the basic principles of behavior. All around us we see other methods used to deal with problematic behavior. Many of these methods are ineffective or counterproductive. The prison system incarcerates the guilty and calls it "punishment," but there is no real evidence that putting people behind bars is actually functional in reducing future incidents of the targeted behaviors. There is evidence that so-called "boot camps" for delinquents are ineffective but they are politically popular and so persist in many communities. Schools operate primarily on the basis of aversive control (loss of recess, detention, paddling, suspension), although we now have nearly thirty years of data showing how positive reinforcement can be used in the classroom to produce truly extraordinary performance gains. Many autistic children, if given the opportunity for behavioral treatment, can make great strides in their socialization and language skills with a significant number joining the mainstream educational

190

system. However, myths persist about the use of special diets, injections of strange substances, and clearly discredited procedures such as facilitated communication (Singer & Lalich, 1996) In clinical psychology, Beutler (2000) has summarized the recent findings this way: "Accumulating evidence indicates that most of the theories and approaches that are used within the community of practitioners are unsupported by empirical evidence of effects" (p. x).

For all of these reasons and more, the BACB® Guidelines prompt behavior analysts to do what they can to promote the application of behavior principles in society as "an alternative approach to treatment and intervention" (Guidelines 10.0 & 10.01). Beyond promoting behavior principles, we encourage consumers to think in terms of empirically-based treatments and data-based decision making. We would truly like our culture to become more scientifically oriented when it comes to understanding human behavior. Opportunities to make this point may come up in habilitation team meetings where some decision is about to be made about treatment, or in conversation with a client about options that are available. Our ethical Guidelines suggest that we look for these opportunities and try to make the best of them without making enemies in the process.

There is a long tradition in psychology of diverting attention from observable behavior to some other level of analysis. A person who smokes is said to have a "need" to smoke or an employee who is non-productive might be said to have a "poor attitude." Our Guideline 10.02, in very simple terms, inspires behavior analysts to keep the focus on "behavior per se" as a focus of our scientific research and presumably our therapy as well. As in promoting the application of behavior principles, this Guideline suggests that we look for opportunities to bring the discussion back to actual behavior, unvarnished with explanatory theories or pseudo scientific, politically correct "psychobabble." Rather than label a child who is "off-task" a great deal of the time as ADHD and refer him to a pediatrician for medication to control his behavior, this Guideline suggests that the behavior analyst, if given the opportunity, should suggest that an analysis of the actual off-task behavior be conducted to determine the functional antecedents, explore the variations in topography, rate, and function, and to seek a practical environmental intervention that can be implemented in the classroom by a competent teacher.

Other responsibilities that behavior analysts have to society include being honest in their public statements and advertising and vigilant to prevent others from misrepresenting behavior analysis practices (Guideline 10.04). We also have an obligation to avoid making false claims about our effectiveness and to ensure that any public statements are factual (Guidelines 10.06 and 10.07).

THE BEHAVIOR ANALYST'S ETHICAL RESPONSIBILITY TO SOCIETY (10.0)

The behavior analyst promotes the general welfare of society through the application of the principles of behavior.

There are many ways in which the behavior analyst can work to improve our society through the ethical application of basic principles of behavior and these Guidelines encourage you to do so.

PROMOTION IN SOCIETY (10.01)

The behavior analyst should promote the application of behavior principles in society by presenting a behavioral alternative to other procedures or methods.

One way of making a difference in society and at the same time promoting the field of behavior analysis is to offer behavioral alternatives to commonly accepted procedures.

CASE EXAMPLE AND QUESTION 102: DR. JUDY N.

Dr. Judy N. is a CBA who consults in DD facilities. Dr. N. has been a lifelong dog lover. Dr. N. got a German shepherd, a breed she has always loved, and shortly thereafter, she purchased a new house. Dr. N. was very dismayed to have her homeowner's insurance company tell her certain breeds of dogs were not insurable by this company and she would have to find a new home for her dog. When she asked why she was told that the company had a policy of not insuring certain breeds because of their "aggressive behavior."

Are there any behavior analytic solutions that Dr. N. can suggest to her insurance agent, and, if necessary, his supervisors?

There are many other examples of how behavior analysts can promote the application of behavioral principles in society. Related to educational settings, one growing trend is to have physically-active children placed on prescription drugs by their pediatricians because of their behavior in school. A behavior analyst working in the schools might have an opportunity to ask if the parents had considered a behavioral alternative.

SCIENTIFIC INQUIRY (10.02)

The behavior analyst should promote the analysis of behavior per se as a legitimate field of scientific inquiry.

If you are given an opportunity to speak or write about behavior analysis, you should take that occasion to point out that behavior analysis is a reasonable and valid approach to understanding human behavior.

CASE EXAMPLE AND QUESTION 103: DR. SCOTT J.

Dr. Scott J. is a BCBA who is an experienced researcher. Dr. J. is active in his neighborhood association and as a neighborhood liaison to local government agencies, he attends city and county com-

mission meetings. The City Commission wants to evaluate the effectiveness of its community programs. City staff members are suggesting survey and statistical research.

In this setting, would it be appropriate for Dr. J. to suggest the use of behavior analysis?

PUBLIC STATEMENTS (10.03)

(a) Behavior analysts comply with these Guidelines in public statements relating to their professional services, products, or publications or to the field of behavior analysis.

It is important to remember that these Guidelines are relevant any time you are communicating with the public about your products, services, or the field of behavior analysis, for example, you must uphold high standards of professional behavior (1.1), maintain confidentiality (2.2.1), not exaggerate your effectiveness (7.1), and acknowledge the contribution of others (7.15).

(b) Public statements include but are not limited to paid or unpaid advertising, brochures, printed matter, directory listings, personal resumes or curriculum vitae, interviews or comments for use in media, statements in legal proceedings, lectures and public oral presentations, and published materials.

Public statements are understood to include any form of advertising, listings in professional directories, publication of your vita, or any form of oral presentation whether in a courtroom, public presentation or in any form of publication.

CASE EXAMPLE AND QUESTION 104A: RENEE

Renee was a CBA who worked in early childhood settings with children born to mothers who were addicted to drugs. A number of the children in the program had also been diagnosed with Fetal Alcohol Syndrome. Renee believed very much in using behavior analysis to help children. When the media called or came to visit the program, they were usually referred to Renee. Renee was an articulate person who had media contacts and she was "camera friendly." From some past training in marketing and public relations, Renee also knew about putting the spin and hype on a media message to get more coverage. In one television interview, to get a lot of attention for the program and for behavior analysis, Renee was quoted as saying, "For these children, behavior analysis offers a miracle. There is no other method of early childhood education that will do what behavior analysis does for these children—it is a proven fact that this population will be successful adults if they have a behavior analysis pre-kindergarten program."

For media purposes, was Renee justified in adding some hype to her message?

STATEMENTS BY OTHERS (10.04)

(a) Behavior analysts who engage others to create or place public statements that promote their professional practice, products, or activities retain professional responsibility for such statements.

If you hire someone to create public statements, you are responsible for what they generate, that is, you are accountable for errors or misstatements.

(b) Behavior analysts make reasonable efforts to prevent others whom they do not control (such as employers, publishers, sponsors, organizational clients, and representatives of the print or broadcast media) from making deceptive statements concerning behavior analysts' practices or professional or scientific activities.

In your professional life, you may find that others, over whom you have no actual influence, may make misleading or dishonest comments about the field of behavior analysis; should this happen, you are required to make sensible effort to prevent or at least manage these remarks or writings.

CASE EXAMPLE AND QUESTION 104B: RENEE

In Case 104a, the early childhood program in which Renee worked continued to receive a lot of media attention. An enthusiastic writer for a women's magazine interviewed Renee over the phone. At the end of the interview the writer told her, "I have a great idea for pitching your story. I see the title of the article as being something like, 'Exciting New Program Cures Crack Babies.' "

It is clear to Renee that the program may get donations and funding as a result of media attention, but she isn't so sure about this magazine's angle. Should she say something?

(c) If behavior analysts learn of deceptive statements about their work made by others, behavior analysts make reasonable efforts to correct such statements.

As described in 7.01 (f), if you learn of misleading or inaccurate statements made about your work, you have an obligation to try and correct them.

(d) A paid advertisement relating to the behavior analyst's activities must be identified as such, unless it is already apparent from the context.

If you develop an ad to place in the newspaper, on the World Wide Web, or on TV, you must clearly label it as a paid advertisement (unless it is obvious).

AVOIDANCE OF FALSE OR DECEPTIVE STATEMENTS (10.05)

Behavior analysts do not make public statements that are false, deceptive, misleading, or fraudulent, either because of what they state, convey, or sug-

gest or because of what they omit, concerning their research, practice, or other work activities or those of persons or organizations with which they are affiliated. Behavior analysts claim as credentials for their behavioral work, only degrees that were primarily or exclusively behavior analytic in content.

Behavior analysts should always tell the truth about their work and about the field. It is inappropriate to cite qualifications other than those in behavior analysis when describing their qualifications in behavior analysis.

CASE EXAMPLE AND QUESTION 105: DR. LILY O.

Dr. Lily O. was a CBA who had worked in DD facilities and group homes for 20 years. A company that managed facilities for clients with head injuries was moving to Dr. O.'s state. She knew there would be several jobs available for behavior analysts in these new facilities. Dr. O. started telling people she knew a lot about the behavioral treatment of head injury and that she would be good at these jobs. In some meetings she attended where she said these things, state level administrators were present. Dr. O. was doing a good sell job for herself and several well-respected people had agreed to write letters of reference.

Dr. O. didn't really lie. She honestly believed she knew a lot about head injury. How do the Guidelines address this?

MEDIA PRESENTATIONS (10.06)

When behavior analysts provide advice or comment by means of public lectures, demonstrations, radio or television programs, prerecorded tapes, printed articles, mailed material, or other media, they take reasonable precautions to ensure that (1) the statements are based on appropriate behavior analytic literature and practice, (2) the statements are otherwise consistent with these Guidelines, and (3) the recipients of the information are not encouraged to infer that a relationship has been established with them personally.

When you are asked to speak publicly on behavior analysis, it is imperative that you make your comments consistent with the research literature and all of these Guidelines (not just this section). It is important that you not convey the impression that you have any individual relationship with viewers or listeners when in fact you do not. (Note: this latter point would be relevant in the case of a radio call-in show, for example.)

CASE EXAMPLE AND QUESTION 106: DR. G.

Dr. G. was a very well known behavior analyst with a great "radio voice" who was occasionally asked to handle questions about behavior problems on a local radio call-in show. He took great pains to remind listeners that what he was suggesting was backed up by empirical research and he gave examples from his own clinical experience to make the show lively and interesting. The show's producer prompted Dr. G. to use the caller's name when giving a reply and to use a "warm tone" to his voice. "Look, all I'm asking you to do is say something like, 'Doug I know exactly what you are talking about and I can understand how you feel and here's what I would do in this case ...' " Dr. G. preferred a more matter-of-fact approach.

Should he have listened to the producer?

TESTIMONIALS (10.07)

Behavior analysts do not solicit testimonials from current clients or patients or other persons who because of their particular circumstances are vulnerable to undue influence.

It is inappropriate for behavior analysts to ask their current clients to issue quotable statements of support on their behalf for the purpose of advertising. To do so might put clients in an awkward position with regard to their current treatment, for example, they might think that they need to be very positive for you to keep treating them. You may wish to ask past clients for a statement of satisfaction with your services, and if you do, you will need to tell them the purpose of the request and how the information will be used. (Note: behavior analysts must always bear in mind the requirement of client confidentiality of information which in most cases would preclude using this type of information.)

CASE EXAMPLE AND QUESTION 107: SANDY C.

Sandy C. was a CABA who worked with med waiver clients. She was a graduate student who was working toward her CBA certification. In Sandy's free time, she enjoyed the hobby of scrapbooking, in which scrapbook pages are elaborately decorated with photos, sayings, clippings, and artwork. Sandy dearly loved her work with clients and decided that she would make a scrapbook about her clients as a sort of keepsake and something she could show her mother when she visited at Thanksgiving. Sandy asked her present clients and some from the recent past to write comments about how she helped them. Sandy artfully put the comments in a scrapbook along with photos of the clients and some cute clip-art that she found online. One day when she was meeting with a case manager for the first time, she showed the case manager her treasured scrapbook as an example of her work.

Was there a problem with this?

IN-PERSON SOLICITATION (10.08)

Behavior analysts do not engage, directly or through agents, in uninvited in-person solicitation of business from actual or potential users of services who because of their particular circumstances are vulnerable to undue influence, except that organizational behavior management or performance management services may be marketed to corporate entities regardless of their projected financial position.

Behavior analysts may, in the course of their daily activities, meet people who clearly need their services. These might be neighbors, business acquaintances, relatives, or individuals in a setting where the behavior analyst is currently consulting or providing treatment, who are in a crisis situation and need immediate help of some sort. To offer services at this time is to take advantage of their stressful situation and is considered highly inappropriate.

CASE EXAMPLE AND QUESTION 108: ROMAN

Roman was a fresh-out-of graduate school CBA who was just establishing himself in a midsized town not far from where he got his degree. He had some new friends and found himself often explaining what he did professionally. On the day that his new business cards came back from the printer, he happened to be standing in line at the grocery store behind a mother with a screaming toddler. She was trying to ignore the child and looked like she was waiting for a break in the crying to try and reinforce some quiet behavior when the cashier pulled out a piece of candy and gave it to the child. The child immediately quit crying, the cashier looked delighted with his quick thinking, and the mother was dumbfounded. Roman reached in his pocket, pulled out a business card, and handed it to the mother saying, "Give me a call; I can help you." When he went through the check-out process, he handed another card to the cashier and said, "I'm not sure that what you did with that child was the right thing to do; give me a call sometime."

Was Roman operating ethically in this situation?

RESPONSES TO CASE QUESTION 102: DR. JUDY N.

Dr. N. has been a responsible dog owner and her dog is now well-trained, thanks to successful operant conditioning procedures. As a behavior analyst, she could try to influence the insurance company's policy by offering to meet with the insurance agent's supervisors, give talks at insurance conferences on dog behavior, dog training, and how behavior analysis can be used as a proven training technique by homeowners to prepare their dogs so that they are safe, nonthreatening, good citizens. Dr. N. could also contact the American Kennel Club and ask for its assistance in lobbying for homeowners' insurance for those homeowners who have taken the extra effort to train their dogs and have them tested for the Canine Good Citizen® certificate that is issued by the American Kennel Club. In other unrelated cases, the behavior analyst could contact the relevant national organization to have an impact.

RESPONSES TO CASE QUESTION 103: DR. SCOTT J.

Behavior analysts should promote the analysis of behavior as a legitimate field of scientific inquiry. Dr. J. can suggest some ways that behavior analytic research can be done to evaluate the effectiveness of community programs.

RESPONSES TO CASE QUESTION 104A: RENEE

Behavior analysts need to comply with the Guidelines in public statements relating to the field of behavior analysis. Renee should not have promised a miracle cure. She also should have not made claims about the long-term ef-

fects of this early childhood program unless the longitudinal research had been done.

RESPONSES TO CASE QUESTION 104B: RENEE

According to the Guidelines, behavior analysts who are working with others to place public statements about behavior analysis are responsible for those statements. Renee should have some assurance that the article will be written and presented in a manner that she can accept, or she should decline the interview. Note that most writers resist the idea that the source (in this case, Renee) will be able to review the article before it goes to print. It would be a good idea for Renee to tape-record the interview (the magazine writer should, of course, be told of the taping) and then, as soon as the phone call is over to review the tape and type up the key quotes she made and send them to the writer. All of this extra work insures that what goes out in print is exactly what Renee said and will prevent her having to try and correct the record after the magazine has come out.

RESPONSES TO CASE QUESTION 105: DR. LILY O.

Behavior analysts do not make false or deceptive statements. By saying she knows a lot about head injury, Dr. O. is implying she has been trained in the area, worked with clients with head injury, and so forth. She needs to be very explicit and say, "I am very interested in this area and would like to learn about it. I am going to see if there is a job that fits with my current skills when the new facility opens."

RESPONSES TO CASE QUESTION 106: DR. G.

Dr. G. has to find the fine balance between being good at the media (if he's not, he'll be fired and won't be able to get the behavior analysis message out) and being ethical. He can take some of the producer's advice to be a little more warm, but he needs to avoid making any statements that suggest he knows more about the caller than he does.

RESPONSES TO CASE QUESTION 107: SANDY C.

The Guidelines state that behavior analysts do not solicit testimonials from clients. Sandy was in violation of the Guidelines both for asking for the letters and showing them to others. Sandy needs to restrict her scrapbooking to topics such as family photos or fun with friends.

RESPONSES TO CASE QUESTION 108: ROMAN

Roman was enthusiastic and evangelistic about his work but way out of line in giving the business card to the mother of the screaming toddler. Giving the card to the cashier was just a waste of time. Roman might consider setting up a meeting with the store manager and telling him of his observation with the cashier (without naming names) and suggest that he could do training for them on basic principles of behavior for the retail setting.

III

Tips and Exercises for Students

A Dozen Practical Tips for Ethical Conduct on Your First Job

As a student, thoughts about ethical problems in your chosen profession probably seem far, far away, and much more theoretical than practical at this point. However, in the not too distant future, perhaps just a few months from now, you will be taking your first job and you will almost immediately begin to confront very real ethical dilemmas, some of which could affect the rest of your professional life. The purpose of this chapter is to outline some common issues that you are likely to encounter early on, and to provide you with some practical tips for dealing with them.

CHOOSING A SETTING OR COMPANY

Your first big decision will involve choosing your first professional position. You might think that the primary considerations involve salary, location, potential for advancement, and matching your professional interests and behavioral skills. All of these are clearly important factors, but one additional choice involves consideration of the ethics and values of the company or organization itself. Currently, behavior analysts are a hot commodity in many places across the country. For some agencies, hiring a BCBA® is essential for funding or to get relief from a federal lawsuit. In such cases, the agency may offer very high starting salaries and extensive benefit packages just to get you on board. Be wary, and ask lots of questions about these positions that appear too good to be true. There is some chance that you will be asked to sign off on programs that you have not written, approve procedures with which you are not familiar, or support agency strategies that are more public relations smoke and mirrors than behavioral methodology. It is appropriate to ask about the history of the agency, company, or organization. Who founded it? What is the overall purpose or mission? How does behavior analysis fit into this mission? Are there any political issues connected with the organization? For example, is this company currently the target of a lawsuit? Are there any "citations" from a recent state or federal survey? How many other behavior analysts are currently employed there? What does the turnover in behavior analysts look like? What is the funding stream? Who are the clients? Who will you be supervising? Are they BCABAs®? Will you be expected to attract and hire CABAs®?

You should be able to discern from the answers, and the way the interviewer handles your questions, whether there might be some ethical problems with the way that the company is run. In a recent case, for example, a small private school for autistic children which had been started by parents and initially headed by a doctoral-level BCBA®, came under some scrutiny by parents and former employees when it was learned that the CBA quit and was not replaced by another CBA. Furthermore, two of the CABAs also left the organization and were not replaced by qualified professionals. The school, which originally attracted parents with its claim of a behavioral approach led by a certified person, still advertised itself as "behaviorally based" and still charged top dollar. It seems clear that going into this organization after more than two years without any behavior analysts could be a very challenging situation where it is likely that your keen awareness of ethical problems will be required. In another case, a rehabilitation facility that was part of a national chain billed itself as behavioral, but hired a nonbehavioral person as the administrator. This is quite common, but in this case, the individual was "subtlety antibehavioral" in her manner in dealing with the CBAs and in her mode of operation. CBAs were told that functional assessments did not need to be done on every client because it was obvious in some cases what the problem was, that data did not need to be taken— it took up too much time—and that she "trusted her staff's impressions" of client progress. In this case, the CBA did not ask enough questions in the initial interview, did not actually meet the administrator who held these views, and was just a little too eager to start bringing home a fat paycheck.

WORKING WITH YOUR SUPERVISOR

In your job interview with the company or organization, it is a good idea to ask to meet your supervisor (this is rarely offered, but an ethical agency will comply if you make the request). Usually you will meet with the administrator, go on a brief tour, perhaps have lunch with some of the professional staff members, and then sit down with someone from the personnel office to negotiate your salary and benefits. However, meeting with the actual person who you will be supervised by and report to is essential if you want to start your first job on a strong ethical foundation. There are many things you want to learn from your potential new supervisor including his or her style—is he or she a reinforcing kind of person, or somewhat negative or withdrawn? Is he or she interested in working with you or does he or she want you do to his or her work? Is there any chance that this person is somewhat jealous of you (you might have a degree from a prestigious, well-known school) and you might be somewhat threatening? Ethically speaking, you would like to be assured that you will not be asked to do anything unethical: (a) you will be able to do your work responsibly; (b) you will have the time and resources to do a great, ethical job; and (c) your supervisor will be there to guide you through troubled waters should the occasion arise. Your supervisor sets the tone for your work: "Just get it done, I don't care how" is far different from "be thorough, get it right, we want what is best for the clients." So, in meeting with your new supervisor, you might ask him or her about his or her philosophy of management, about the most difficult ethical issue he or she has encountered in the last year, and how he or she handled it. Or, you might ask about any ethical issues you might encounter in your work. Just an open-ended question here should start the conversation going and you can carry it from there with follow-up questions. When you're finished with this interview, you should have a secure, optimistic feeling about working for this person. If you feel apprehensive, think twice about taking the position, even if it is more money you ever thought you'd see in a first job.

LEARN JOB EXPECTATIONS UP FRONT

If you have followed our suggestions up to this point, you will be happy and excited about your new position as a professional behavior analyst, making great money, and helping people. Before you get too carried away, it would be a good idea to clarify exactly what you are supposed to do on a day-to-day basis. In your first three months on any job, you have a sort of grace period where you can ask questions without appearing to be dumb. If you are going to be analyzing behavior, doing functional assessments, writing programs, and training staff, you should be well prepared from your graduate work. However, each agency and organization has its own method for doing each of these tasks. Your first assignment is to find out how administrators want it done. So, ask for copies of "exemplary" intake interviews, case work-ups, functional assessments, and behavioral programs. You can avoid embarrassing and potentially ethically challenging situations if you know how your new consulting firm routinely handles complaints from consumers, inquiries from review committees, and issues with state agencies. You can make sure that your ethical standards match the other professionals if you review minutes of habilitation-team meetings and take a look at behavior programs written by previous behavior analysts. You might also want to know in advance if you are expected to chair the weekly case review meetings or simply attend, and whether, in these meetings, there is open discussion of ethical issues. One of the most important job-related ethical issues involves whether you will be working within your level of competence or whether you will be asked to take on cases or tasks for which you are not fully qualified.

One newly-minted BCBA joined some others in a mental health facility where she was assigned to the retarded-defendant program for which she was highly qualified. After a few weeks, she was asked to do some IQ testing on some mental health patients, on short notice, and under short deadline pressure. She had avoided taking intelligence-testing classes in graduate school and pointed this skill deficiency out to her supervisor along with a question about why this requirement was not mentioned in the job interview. Then she pointed out how the BACB® Guidelines discourage behavior analysts from working out of their area. In some cases, this can brand a person as "not a team player," but really it is an ethical issue. Even if she did do the testing, it wouldn't be valid, and what if someone made a decision based on the test scores? This would surely be unethical. So, to avoid situations like this one, make sure that you ask plenty of questions early on, in the job interview and once you've started work, about what is expected, and establish the ethical boundaries necessary to protect yourself from engaging in unethical behavior.

DON'T GET IN OVER YOUR HEAD

Most people just starting out on their first job are excited to be doing what they've dreamed about for years: practicing behavior analysis as a professional and making a difference in people's lives. Early on you are likely to be so grateful to have a job that you will do nearly anything to please your supervisor and upper level management. Your enthusiasm could actually cause some harm, however, if it turns out that you take on more than you can handle or take on cases without some recognition of their difficulty. Your most important goal is to do a first-class job on each and every case that you are assigned. If you put your heart and soul into your work, and watch out for conflicts of interest and "do no harm," you will be fine. But, if you take on too many cases, then the next thing that will happen is that something falls through the cracks and clients start complaining, or your supervisor notices that your reports are sloppy, or the peer review committee starts making negative comments about your programs. In behavior analysis, doing more is not always associated with doing better. Quality counts. This is especially the case because you are affecting the life of a person with your work. You owe it to your clients as well as yourself to take only the number of cases that you can do well.

This same philosophy holds for taking on cases for which you have no expertise. In your training, you may not have worked at all with clients who are sex offenders, or who are mentally ill, or who are profoundly physically disabled. You do not do yourself or the client any favors by taking these cases. You will no doubt be under a lot of pressure to do so from parents, teachers, or program administrators, but if you just think of the harm that could be done by your taking a case and then handling it badly, you will think twice about this decision. The easiest, and most ethical stance to take is to always work within your range of competence. If you want to increase your range, the proper thing to do is to find another professional to serve as your mentor, someone who can give you proper training. You may also want to consider taking additional graduate coursework in a certain specialty area in addition to doing some practicum with supervision from an expert in that area.

USING DATA FOR DECISION MAKING

One of the distinguishing characteristics of the profession of behavior analysis is the reliance on data collection and data analysis. For us data counts. The Florida Association for Behavior Analysis has a new motto, "got data?" that is now available on Tee shirts, coffee mugs, and keychains as a takeoff on the milk producers' "got milk?" campaign. If there is anything that distinguishes us from other human services professionals, it is that we have a strong ethic in favor of objective data (not anecdotal, not self-report, not questionnaire) on individual behavior and the use of this data to evaluate the effects of treatments we devise and implement. Technically speaking, it is unethical to start an intervention without baseline data. And, it is unethical to continue a treatment without taking more data to see if it was effective. Most behavior analysts agree to this and, although it is procedural, it is written into our code of ethics (BACB Guidelines, 4.04). So, as long as you are taking data and using it to evaluate a procedure, you are ethically in the clear, right? Well, not exactly. It is actually a little more complicated than this. First of all, as you know, there is data and then there is *data*. The latter is reliable (meaning reliability checks that are carried out under specified conditions with a second, independent, observer, and reach a certain standard) and socially validated (meaning that standards of social validity have been met, again under specified conditions). It can be argued that a practicing behavior analyst not only has to take data to be ethical but that the data has to be reliable and valid; after all, there is a lot riding on the data: treatment decisions, medication decisions, retain or discharge decisions. As an ethical behavior analyst, you would not want to use data that was tainted by observer bias, or which had a reliability of, say fifty percent. Furthermore, you wouldn't want to make treatment decisions if you thought the data had no social validity. So, what do you do as an ethical behavior analyst? You carry a burden to not only be data based in your decision making but to assure the client, client surrogates, and your peers that you have quality data (again, not self-report, not anecdotal, not questionnaire).

One final issue about the use of data in decision making; this has to do with whether your treatment was in fact responsible for any behavior change. Again, to be ethical, it would appear that it is your responsibility to know in a functional sense that it was your treatment that worked and not some outside or coincidental variable. This suggests that as a practical, ethical matter you should be looking for ways of demonstrating experimental control either with a reversal or multiple-baseline design. If you put in a treatment and the behavior changes, you cannot in all honesty say it was your intervention because you don't really know this for sure. Right about the time you instituted your treatment plan the physician could have made a medication change, or the client may have developed an illness, or gotten some bad news, or perhaps someone else put in an intervention about the same time without your knowledge (e.g., the dietician cut back the person's calories, the client's roommate kept him up most of the night, etc.). In summary, as an ethical behavior analyst, you are obligated to be data based in your decision making and to develop a high quality data collection system that allows you to address issues of reliability, validity, and demonstrations of experimental control. You will find that professionals in other areas don't take all of these issues into consideration and you should be proud to be part of a profession that takes data so seriously.

TRAINING AND SUPERVISING OTHERS

As a behavior analyst, you are probably already aware that others, usually paraprofessionals, who are trained by you, do much of the actual behavior treatment. Your job as the behavior analyst is to take the referral, qualify it to make sure it falls into the behavioral problem area (as opposed to being a nursing problem or education issue, for example), and then perform an appropriate functional assessment to determine likely causes of the behavior. Once this is determined, you will draw up a behavior program, based on empirically-tested, published, interventions, and then train someone to carry out the interventions. The ethical burden here is that you have to not only do the functional assessment according to accepted protocols, but also that you have to properly train the parents, teachers, residential staff, aides, or others. You are ultimately responsible for the program's effectiveness. This means that the program is carried out to your specifications. We know from the research literature that some methods of training work and some don't. The most reliable form of training is not to simply give the parent a written program and then ask, "Are there any questions?" It is also not acceptable to explain the program and then leave a written copy. It is far more effective, and ethical, if you demonstrate the procedure, then have the parents practice, then provide feedback, have them try again, and so on until they do it right. Then you give them a written copy, and maybe a videotape just to make sure, and then you may leave, but only for a short time because you need to make a spot check a few days later to observe and see if they are doing it right. If not, you will need to do some correction, some more role-play, and some more feedback, and then another visit a few days later. This is ethical training. Anything less is unethical.

Probably within six months of taking your first job, you will be supervising others (in some positions it may be immediate). As a behavior analyst, you again have a high standard to meet in terms of the quality of your supervision. Because we have such an extensive literature on ways of changing behavior in the workplace (in fact, there is a whole subspecialty called *Performance Management*), you now have an ethical obligation to be an effective supervisor. It's not all that difficult for a person steeped in basic behavior analysis procedures. First, make sure you use the most effective antecedents. Don't lecture, demonstrate. After the demonstration, ask your supervisees to show you what they've learned. Then give immediate positive feedback. If you are training on written materials, for example, how to prepare a behavior program, show your trainee a sample of the best program that you can find. If necessary, break the task into smaller "bites" of material. And, consider using backward chaining if necessary. Practice giving positive reinforcement for work you see and receive every day, many times a day. You will soon discover that your supervisees and trainees seek you out for advice and assistance; they will want to show you their work and get your approval. If you are working in a large organization, you could easily become the most reinforcing person there without even trying hard. The time will come when you do have to give negative feedback or show disapproval. If you've worked hard to give out contingent reinforcers, the person who receives this punisher will initially be somewhat shocked (he or she might have gotten the initial impression that you were just a "goody-two-shoes"). Remember, the purpose of this correction is to change behavior, not punish the person, so you will also want to keep reinforcing the appropriate behavior. And, don't forget your autoclitics (Skinner's *Verbal Behavior,* chap. 12, 1957), those little comments that mean so much when you have to give someone negative feedback. "You know that I value what you do, and that your work here has been excellent, now let me just point out something that is not quite right in this behavior program ...." One of the best books that can be used as a basic primer for business and professional skills is Dale Carnegie's *How to Win Friends and Influence People* (1981). You should review this little gem as a supplement to what you have learned about behavioral supervision.

TIME KEEPING FOR BILLING AND SUPERVISION

An essential part of professional ethics is accountability. One of the most important aspects of accountability is that you keep track of how you spend your time. Time is your primary commodity. For your first position, you may find that you are working on a "billable hour" model of compensation. In this system, the agency or consulting firm you are working for has contracted for your services at a certain rate per hour and every documented hour that you work can be billed. You then receive a biweekly or monthly check based on your total number of billable hours. Although it may seem like a small matter, keep consistent, precise records of each and every billable unit—usually a quarter hour. Do not rely on your memory at the end of the day to reconstruct your activities and do not average them out over a week. You will probably be able to set up a file on your PDA that will allow you to note for each client the date, time, and duration of contact as well as a brief note of what you did. At the end of the billing cycle, all you then need to do is perform a few simple calculations to determine your billing to the agency or consulting firm. One important feature of this accounting is that you understand how critical it is to your firm that you actually match your hours of service to the contracted hours. If your agency or consulting firm has contracted with a facility for you to spend twenty hr per week on-site, it is inappropriate for you to only provide sixteen hr of service. First, the determination was made by the facility and your consulting firm that twenty hr was needed. The facility has set aside a certain amount of money for your services and they have mutually agreed that they need twenty hr of consulting or therapy. For you to decide on your own to take a day off is inappropriate and constitutes a violation of BACB Guidelines 2.03 and 6.01.

Needless to say, accurate and honest time accountability is essential to protect you from any allegation that you have been overbilling or that you have attempted to defraud a client or the government. This is especially urgent because there are cases being prosecuted at a high rate of physicians who are billing for clients they do not see or for services that are never rendered.

A related issue pertains to the need to keep close track not only of your billable hours but also your supervision hours. Many behavior analysts who take their first job after graduation are in need of hours of supervised experience to take the CBA exam. The same procedure described earlier for billable hours is used to keep track of the service hours you have completed and an accompanying record of the number of hours of supervision that you have received. You should not rely on your supervisor to keep track of this data; it is your responsibility. Note in particular that you are required to complete either eighteen months of "mentored" experience or nine months of "supervised" experience and that this must be in units of at least twenty hr per week (i.e., at least a half-time job) for eighty hr per month. Many graduate school part-time positions are only sixteen hr per week; if you were attempting to meet the requirement, you would then need to do at least four additional hr per week of pro bono work to meet the total of twenty hr. It is clear that you will need to document this so that at the end of your mentored or supervised experience, there is no doubt as to whether you have met the requirement.

WATCH FOR CONFLICTS OF INTEREST

One of the most subtle unethical problems that can develop for any professional is that of a conflict of interest. Much is made in the clinical literature of the problem of the psychotherapist having sex with clients either during or after therapy as a prime example of a conflict of interest and exploitation of a vulnerable person (the client) by a more powerful person (the therapist). Another example is the therapist developing some sort of business or social relationship with a client or former client such as hiring that person to do work around the house or garden. In these cases, it is easy to see that such a relationship in our field could "impair the behavior analyst's objectivity" and affect his or her decision making. It would be a bad idea, for example, to take as a client someone you know, such as a friend, neighbor, or relative.

In behavior analysis, there are other relationships that could be problematic that appear to be unique to our field. Behavior analysts are not restricted to the role of therapist. They are also supervisors, consultants, teachers, and researchers. Behavior analysts may sit on local or state-wide human rights committees or peer-review committees. They may own a consulting firm or be an elected member of a professional association. The role of behavior therapist is also complicated by the fact that some therapy may be done in the home of the client as in discrete-trial therapy with autistic children. In this case, the family of the child client may develop a stronger bond with the behavior analyst than would be the case if the sessions were conducted in a clinic or at school. It has been reported often that parents under these circumstances begin to see the therapist as part of the family and will want to include them on outings or invite them to birthday parties or other family events. Surely participating in such events would begin to "impair the behavior analyst's objectivity" and serve as a prime example of a conflict of interest when the time came to give an objective account of the child's progress or for a recommendation to be made to terminate the case. Serving on a peer-review committee where you are supposed to render an impartial judgment about the quality of a treatment program could present an objectivity problem if a friend or former student developed the case being presented. An owner of a consulting firm has a built-in conflict of interest when considering accepting a new client; the potential income from the case may cloud the judgment of the owner from determining that it would be in the client's best interest to refer to another behavior analyst who has more expertise with a special behavior problem. Of course, the same conflict exists at the individual therapist level when he or she must decide to take a client who has been referred. Decisions in all these cases revolve around the question of what is in the client's best interest (BACB Guideline 2.0: "The behavior analyst has a responsibility to operate in the best interest of clients") rather than what would benefit the therapist, the consulting firm, or the agency.

FIND A "TRUSTED COLLEAGUE" RIGHT AWAY

It is difficult to make ethical decisions in isolation. Without a sounding board, what appears to you to be an easy call may in fact be quite a complex dilemma. Determining whether some harm might come from a particular intervention is not that easy to establish in many cases. The effects could be delayed or subtle and someone else with more experience than you could be a big help in making such a decision. Over time, you will feel more confident about your behavioral decisions but in the beginning, to help build your confidence, we strongly recommend that you find a "trusted colleague" as soon as possible. Ideally this would be another behavior analyst who is easily accessible and who is not your supervisor or your employer. For political and other reasons, the colleague probably should not work for "the competition" in your geographical area. Your trusted colleague is someone that you will entrust some rather deep thoughts of yours such as, (a) "Am I really prepared to take this case? " or, (b) "My supervisor is telling me do to X but it seems unethical to me. What should I do?" or even more important, (c) "I think I've made a big mistake, what do I do now?" With luck you won't encounter any of these dilemmas in your first three months on the job and you can use this time to try and find a person who is knowledgeable and who you can trust. In your off hours, your first three months on the job should be spent interacting with other professionals from your workplace and in your general locale. It's a good idea to get to know social workers, nurses, physicians, case managers, psychologists, and client advocates, as well as any other behavior analysts in your area. This networking will serve other purposes also, such as making referrals; in this process of getting to know your colleagues you should make the acquaintance of someone who can be more than a casual business associate and become a confidant. You will want to size up this person's approach to ethics and make sure that his or her approach to dealing with complex issues appears to be sound, thoughtful, and deliberate, not glib or cavalier. A CBA with five or more years of experience who is careful in what she does, has a good solid reputation, and who seems friendly and approachable, would be a good candidate. You want to find your trusted colleague well before anything "hits the fan" because you will want to have a well-established rapport with the person and feel confident that you can in fact trust him or her with your urgent ethical situation.

TOUCHING PEOPLE

Unlike ordinary office-based psychotherapy, behavior analysis often involves getting up close and personal with your clients. Especially for those behavior analysts working with the developmentally-disabled, the physically-challenged, and the behavior-disordered client, our treatments may involve touching or holding the person. Innocuous procedures like graduated guidance involve putting your hands on the client to help him or her learn how to do some task like self-feeding or dressing. Toilet training can involve helping the person remove his or her clothes and tooth brushing requires the behavior analyst to stand behind the client and help manipulate the brush. Many behavior analysts routinely give "hugs" or brief shoulder massages as reinforcers without thinking of the possible adverse consequences. In all of these cases, even the most benign and well-intentioned action on your part could be misconstrued or misinterpreted as "inappropriate touching." This accusation could come from the client, the client's parents, a nearby caregiver, or even a visitor who just happened to be on the scene. Other more intrusive behavioral procedures are even more problematic: time-out almost always involves holding the client while taking him or her to the time-out room. Manual restraint, or attempting to apply mechanical restraints, can also present issues of potential misinterpretation or misperception (from "You hurt me," to "You hurt him deliberately," to "Were you groping her? I think you were, you pervert, I'm going to call the police!").

The ethical behavior analyst will always abide by the dictum "do no harm," and will avoid at all costs doing anything to in any way physically or emotionally harm a client. But, the cautious, ethical behavior analyst will also make sure that he or she is never the target of a mistaken or malicious accusation of physically inappropriate behavior toward a client. To this end, we make the following recommendations: (a) to avoid a false client allegation of inappropriate touching, always make sure to have another person (often called a "witness") present; (b) make sure the witness knows what you are doing and why you are doing it; (c) if you are involved in any sort of physical restraint use, make sure that you have been properly trained and certified to do so; (d) if you know of a client who has a history of false reports of inappropriate touching, be wary of close contact with that person unless you have done (a) and (b), discussed earlier; and finally, (e) avoid cross-sex therapeutic interactions (male therapist–female client) unless there is absolutely no alternative (you will still want to follow rule (a) and (b), however). The purpose of these recommendations is not to encourage you to become cold and impersonal in your interactions with clients, but rather to promote some thinking about how your warm and affectionate behavior might backfire on you.

DEALING WITH NONBEHAVIORAL COLLEAGUES

Most of your professional time will be spent with colleagues who are not behavior analysts. Depending on the setting and the history of the agency or organization, this could present you with some serious ethical dilemmas. For example, if as part of a habilitation team you find that the consensus of the group is that your client should receive "counseling," you have an ethical obligation to propose a behavioral alternative (BACB Guideline 10.01) and to raise questions about whether there is any data on treatment efficacy (BACB Guideline 2.09 [a]) for "counseling." This could make you somewhat unpopular on the team. Furthermore, if this treatment is actually implemented you have an obligation to request that data be taken to evaluate it (BACB Guideline 2.09 [c]). To make matters worse, if you are ethical in following these guidelines, you are likely to be in the spotlight when it comes time to evaluate your proposed interventions, so you will have to be ready with copies of studies to justify your treatments and be scrupulous about taking objective and accurate data to determine if they in fact work with this client.

You may soon discover that the other professionals with which you deal are not very aware of the ethics code for their field or pay it little heed. Or worse, you may discover that their code of ethics is not very clear on issues regarding client's rights, use of empirically-based procedures, or the evaluation of treatments using data. New students working in the field for the first time are often shocked at the cavalier way in which meetings are conducted and decisions are made regarding clients. It is not unusual for one person to dominate the meetings with a clear motive of getting it over with as soon as possible. Often there is no data presented and weak or no rationales given for pushing certain treatment approaches. Convenience, a "just go along" attitude, and disregard for ethics in general, is often the mode for these meetings that appear to be held more for show than for function. Initially, as a new and probably junior member of the treatment team, you will probably want to sit quietly and observe; try to determine who is in charge and what the custom is for handling decision making. You may need to consult with your supervisor about how best to handle these situations and consult the BACB code of ethics for some key foundation points. Before you accuse anyone in public of engaging in unethical conduct, it would be wise to again check with your supervisor and then possibly meet with the professional in question outside of the meetings to discuss your concerns. This may also be a time for you to consult with your trusted colleague. In extreme cases, where you and your supervisor feel that you have done everything possible to have some impact but have been unsuccessful, it may be necessary to terminate your involvement. Guidelines 2.14 (a–d) address the circumstances for such a dramatic move and describe how this should be done.

So, to end on a positive note, it is important to point out that the vast majority of nonbehavioral colleagues are kind and caring, mean well, and will tolerate you if you will tolerate them. Most have never heard of behavior analysis, so you will have a chance to be an ambassador for the field and to educate them about current developments and how we are, in the utmost, concerned about the ethical, effective, and humane treatment of clients. Be patient with them and give them a chance to educate you about their field. Be a good listener and a positive supportive person and you will grow immeasurably as a professional yourself. Be honest about your own shortcomings (e.g., you may know very little about medications and how they work with certain behaviors) and open to other points of view. Over time, you will gain some perspective on how others view behavior and understand how you can nudge them toward a more behavioral perspective.

SEXUAL HARASSMENT

Sexual harassment is one of those awkward, ugly topics that few people want to discuss unless pressed to do so. Despite years of education, legal rulings, and company fines, it still exists (United States Equal Employment Opportunity Commission, 2003). As a behavior analyst, you might think that you might never be subject to this kind of treatment by others. Although you would never intentionally treat another person in this degrading way, nonetheless, there are a few behavioral aspects of sexual harassment that should be discussed for the new behavior analyst.

First, we need to address unwanted sexual advances. If you have some special work circumstances, you might be more likely to encounter this problem. CBAs who work in the client's home may find that there are occasions when they are alone with a single parent of the opposite sex (young female therapists seem most vulnerable if there is a divorced or single male in the house). It can start innocently enough with the person acting very interested in your work, perhaps sitting close, making exceptionally good eye contact, or smiling a lot. And, you might take this as just a very involved person who thinks that you and your work are fascinating. An extra warm greeting, a hug that lasts just a little longer than it should, or a touch to the arm or shoulder, are the first clues that there may be something else afoot here. Behavior analysts are trained to be superb observers of behavior and this is the skill that you want to bring to bear at this time. Behavior analysts also know how to use DRO, punish behaviors, put them on extinction, or bring them under stimulus control to reduce their rate of occurrence. So, if you detect the early stages of unusually "familiar" behaviors, it is time to swing into action. Step one is to monitor your own behavior closely to make sure that you are not sending out any improper signals that advances might be welcome. This can be very difficult for a behavior analyst because another aspect of your training no doubt involved becoming a big reinforcer for those around you, particularly your clients; this can easily be misconstrued as your having a personal interest in the individual. Having determined that you are not in any way encouraging the person, you need to begin working on ways of decreasing the behavior. You might use DRO by reinforcing the person for sitting a little further away from you; for any "romantic" eye-contact responses, look at the floor or at your paperwork, appear distracted or abruptly conclude the meeting. Inappropriate touching can be handled with a "cold stare" with no smiling and possibly a no-nonsense, "That's really not appropriate, Mr. Applegate." If you have caught this in the early stages and these tentative behaviors are punished, your problem may be solved. If it has gone further than this, and the person is very inappropriate (such as calling you at home or leaving personal e-mail messages), you need to make sure that you've got your extinction procedures memorized and are ready to put them into action. The prime foe of the victim of sexual harassment is intermittent reinforcement. If the person is calling you at home, and you decide to use extinction, you will need to screen your calls and never pick up for these calls. Using extinction for a week and then in frustration picking up the phone to say, "I really don't want to talk to you, please don't call me here," is probably the worst thing you can do because, in point of fact, you just reinforced his or her making a run of twenty-five calls. When you start extinction, you must follow through. And you have to realize from your reading of the research literature that the behavior will probably escalate in some way (frequency, intensity, topography); be prepared to withstand this increase and know that seeing such escalation is a sign that perhaps extinction is beginning to work. Non-behaviorally-trained people can be forgiven for making reinforcement, punishment, and extinction mistakes but as a "Board Certified" behavior analyst, you have no excuse for not applying what you know to solve a serious personal problem like this one.

The second major concern regarding sexual harassment is the possibility that you will be accused by someone else of this behavior. We specifically train behavior analysts to be effective interpersonally and this includes using head nodding, smiling, warm handshakes, strong, effective verbal reinforcers, and so on. We encourage new consultants to "become a reinforcer" for those around you if you want to be effective. Different reinforcing behaviors are appropriate in different settings. In business and organizational settings, smiling, handshakes, and positive comments are all appropriate; on the shop floor, a pat on the back or shoulder hug might be acceptable. But, you need to be careful that those you are "reinforcing" don't get the wrong idea and think that you are attracted to them. You might be working with a withdrawn child, for example, and trying to get her to stay on task or complete an assignment. At the first sign of success you break into a smile, give "high fives," and then a hug. Over time, this will probably work to increase the on-task behavior but you may begin to also increase your rate of hugs or they may become a little more enthusiastic. The next thing you know you get called into the principal's office and she says, "I've just gotten off the phone with little Lucy's mother. Lucy has complained that you touched her in her private areas. Is this true?"

The best advice to new behavior analysts is to be courteous, polite, even charming, but in all cases be professional. Do not let your enthusiasm for the progress of your client overwhelm you, or the excitement of meeting a goal prompt you to get overly emotional and all "touchy-feely" with a client. Watch what you do with your hands at all times. As a check on your performance, ask yourself, "What if Channel Six Eyewitness News was here taping this? Would I still engage in this behavior?" If the answer is "no," then you need to modify your own behavior to prevent any misunderstanding or false accusations.

A FINAL NOTE

Most behavior analysts get so caught up in the intense minute-to-minute practice of their profession that it is difficult to stop and ask, "Is there an ethical problem here?" You might be caught off guard at the grocery store by someone who wants to know something about another client. It starts off innocently enough but then the inappropriate question slips out: "I saw you working with Jimmy C., Marge's little boy. Why are you working with him?" Or, you are working hard to please your new supervisor and are right at your limit when she asks you to "drop everything and take charge of this, now." Your tendency is to do what you are told, to try and be a compliant worker. But the task might be out of your range of competence or it might be unethical ("Bring your bottle of white-out, we've got to fix some records, the review team is due here tomorrow …").

It is hoped that this volume will help you think about ethics not in a theoretical or purely moral sense but rather in the practical sense of doing the right thing, doing no harm, being just, truthful, fair, and responsible, affording dignity to your clients, promoting their independence, and in general, treating others the way that you would like to be treated. The world would surely be a better place if everyone adopted the behavior analyst's ethical principles and put them to practical use every day.

Behavior Analyst Certification Board® Guidelines for Responsible Conduct For Behavior Analysts (August 2004)

1.0 RESPONSIBLE CONDUCT OF A BEHAVIOR ANALYST.

The behavior analyst maintains the high standards of professional behavior of the professional organization.

1.01 Reliance on Scientific Knowledge.

Behavior analysts rely on scientifically and professionally derived knowledge when making scientific or professional judgments in human service provision, or when engaging in scholarly or professional endeavors.

1.02 Competence and Professional Development.

The behavior analyst remains proficient in professional practice and the performance of professional functions by reading the appropriate literature, attending conferences and conventions, participating in workshops, and/or obtaining Behavior Analyst Certification Board certification.

1.03 Competence.

(a) Behavior analysts provide services, teach, and conduct research only within the boundaries of their competence, based on their education, training, supervised experience, or appropriate professional experience.

(b) Behavior analysts provide services, teach, or conduct research in new areas or involving new techniques only after first undertaking appropriate study, training, supervision, and/or consultation from persons who are competent in those areas or techniques.

1.04 Professional Development.

Behavior analysts who engage in assessment, therapy, teaching, research, organizational consulting, or other professional activities maintain a reasonable level of awareness of current scientific and professional information in their fields of activity, and undertake ongoing efforts to maintain competence in the skills they use.

1.05 Integrity.

(a) The behavior analyst's behavior conforms to the legal and moral codes of the social and professional community of which the behavior analyst is a member.

(b) The activity of a behavior analyst falls under these Guidelines only if the activity is part of his or her work-related functions or the activity is behavior analytic in nature.

(c) If behavior analysts' ethical responsibilities conflict with law, behavior analysts make known their commitment to these Guidelines and take steps to resolve the conflict in a responsible manner in accordance with law.

1.06 Professional and Scientific Relationships.

(a) Behavior analysts provide behavioral diagnostic, therapeutic, teaching, research, supervisory, consultative, or other behavior analytic services only in the context of a defined, remunerated professional or scientific relationship or role.

(b) When behavior analysts provide assessment, evaluation, treatment, counseling, supervision, teaching, consultation, research, or other behavior analytic services to an individual, a group, or an organization, they use language that is fully understandable to the recipient of those services. They provide appropriate information prior to service delivery about the nature of such services and appropriate information later about results and conclusions.

(c) Where differences of age, gender, race, ethnicity, national origin, religion, sexual orientation, disability, language, or socioeconomic status significantly affect behavior analysts' work concerning particular individuals or groups, behavior analysts obtain the training, experience, consultation, or supervision necessary to ensure the competence of their services, or they make appropriate referrals.

(d) In their work-related activities, behavior analysts do not engage in discrimination against individuals or groups based on age, gender, race, ethnicity, national origin, religion, sexual orientation, disability, socioeconomic status, or any basis proscribed by law.

(e) Behavior analysts do not knowingly engage in behavior that is harassing or demeaning to persons with whom they interact in their work based on factors such as those persons' age, gender, race, ethnicity, national origin, religion, sexual orientation, disability, language, or socioeconomic status, in accordance with law.

(f) Behavior analysts recognize that their personal problems and conflicts may interfere with their effectiveness. Behavior analysts refrain from providing services when their personal circumstances may compromise delivering services to the best of their abilities.

1.07 Dual Relationships.

(a) In many communities and situations, it may not be feasible or reasonable for behavior analysts to avoid social or other nonprofessional contacts with persons such as clients, students, supervisees, or research participants. Behavior analysts must always be sensitive to the potential harmful effects of other contacts on their work and on those persons with whom they deal.

(b) A behavior analyst refrains from entering into or promising a personal, scientific, professional, financial, or other relationship with any such person if it appears likely that such a relationship reasonably might impair the behavior analyst's objectivity or otherwise interfere with the behavior analyst's ability to effectively perform his or her functions as a behavior analyst, or might harm or exploit the other party.

(c) If a behavior analyst finds that, due to unforeseen factors, a potentially harmful multiple relationship has arisen (i.e., one in which the reasonable possibility of conflict of interest or undue influence is present), the behavior analyst attempts to resolve it with due regard for the best interests of the affected person and maximal compliance with these Guidelines.

1.08 Exploitative Relationships.

(a) Behavior analysts do not exploit persons over whom they have supervisory, evaluative, or other authority such as students, supervisees, employees, research participants, and clients.

(b) Behavior analysts do not engage in sexual relationships with clients, students, or supervisees in training over whom the behavior analyst has evaluative or direct authority, because such relationships easily impair judgment or become exploitative.

(c) Behavior analysts are cautioned against bartering with clients because it is often (1) clinically contraindicated, and (2) prone to formation of an exploitative relationship.

2.0 THE BEHAVIOR ANALYST'S RESPONSIBILITY TO CLIENTS.

The behavior analyst has a responsibility to operate in the best interest of clients.

2.01 Definition of Client.

The term client as used here is broadly applicable to whomever the behavior analyst provides services whether an individual person (service recipient), parent or guardian of a service recipient, an institutional representative, a public or private agency, a firm or corporation.

2.02 Responsibility.

The behavior analyst's responsibility is to all parties affected by behavioral services.

2.03 Consultation.

(a) Behavior analysts arrange for appropriate consultations and referrals based principally on the best interests of their clients, with appropriate consent, and subject to other relevant considerations, including applicable law and contractual obligations.

(b) When indicated and professionally appropriate, behavior analysts cooperate with other professionals in order to serve their clients effectively and appropriately. Behavior analysts recognize that other professions have ethical codes that may differ in their specific requirements from of these Guidelines.

2.04 Third-Party Requests for Services.

(a) When a behavior analyst agrees to provide services to a person or entity at the request of a third party, the behavior analyst clarifies to the extent feasible, at the outset of the service, the nature of the relationship with each party. This clarification includes the role of the behavior analyst (such as therapist, organizational consultant, or expert witness), the probable uses of the services provided or the information obtained, and the fact that there may be limits to confidentiality.

(b) If there is a foreseeable risk of the behavior analyst being called upon to perform conflicting roles because of the involvement of a third party, the behavior analyst clarifies the nature and direction of his or her responsibilities, keeps all parties appropriately informed as matters develop, and resolves the situation in accordance with these Guidelines.

2.05 Rights and Prerogatives of Clients.

(a) The behavior analyst supports individual rights under the law.

(b) The client must be provided on request an accurate, current set of the behavior analyst's credentials.

(c) Permission for electronic recording of interviews is secured from clients and all other settings. Consent for different uses must be obtained specifically and separately.

(d) Clients must be informed of their rights, and about procedures to complain about professional practices of the behavior analyst.

2.06 Maintaining Confidentiality.

(a) Behavior analysts have a primary obligation and take reasonable precautions to respect the confidentiality of those with whom they work or consult, recognizing that confidentiality may be established by law, institutional rules, or professional or scientific relationships.

(b) Clients have a right to confidentiality. Unless it is not feasible or is contraindicated, the discussion of confidentiality occurs at the outset of the relationship and thereafter as new circumstances may warrant.

(c) In order to minimize intrusions on privacy, behavior analysts include only information germane to the purpose for which the communication is made in written and oral reports, consultations, and the like.

(d) Behavior analysts discuss confidential information obtained in clinical or consulting relationships, or evaluative data concerning patients, individual or organizational clients, students, research participants, supervisees, and employees, only for appropriate scientific or professional purposes and only with persons clearly concerned with such matters.

2.07 Maintaining Records.

Behavior analysts maintain appropriate confidentiality in creating, storing, accessing, transferring, and disposing of records under their control, whether these are written, automated, or in any other medium. Behavior analysts maintain and dispose of records in accordance with applicable federal or state law or regulation, and corporate policy, and in a manner that permits compliance with the requirements of these Guidelines.

2.08 Disclosures.

(a) Behavior analysts disclose confidential information without the consent of the individual only as mandated by law, or where permitted by law for a valid purpose, such as (1) to provide needed professional services to the individual or organizational client, (2) to obtain appropriate professional consultations, (3) to protect the client or others from harm, or (4) to obtain payment for services, in which instance disclosure is limited to the minimum that is necessary to achieve the purpose.

(b) Behavior analysts also may disclose confidential information with the appropriate consent of the individual or organizational client (or of another legally authorized person on behalf of the client), unless prohibited by law.

2.09 Treatment Efficacy.

(a) The behavior analyst always has the responsibility to recommend scientifically supported most effective treatment procedures. Effective treatment procedures have been validated as having both long-term and short-term benefits to clients and society.

(b) Clients have a right to effective treatment (i.e., based on the research literature and adapted to the individual client).

(c) Behavior analysts are responsible for review and appraisal of likely effects of all alternative treatments, including those provided by other disciplines and no intervention.

2.10 DOCUMENTING PROFESSIONAL AND SCIENTIFIC WORK.

(a) Behavior analysts appropriately document their professional and scientific work in order to facilitate provision of services later by them or by other professionals, to ensure accountability, and to meet other requirements of institutions or the law.

(b) When behavior analysts have reason to believe that records of their professional services will be used in legal proceedings involving recipients of or participants in their work, they have a responsibility to create and maintain documentation in the kind of detail and quality that would be consistent with reasonable scrutiny in an adjudicative forum.

2.11 Records and Data.

Behavior analysts create, maintain, disseminate, store, retain, and dispose of records and data relating to their research, practice, and other work in accordance with applicable federal and state laws or regulations and corporate policy and in a manner that permits compliance with the requirements of these Guidelines.

2.12 Fees and Financial Arrangements.

(a) As early as is feasible in a professional or scientific relationship, the behavior analyst and the client or other appropriate recipient of behavior analytic services reach an agreement specifying the compensation and the billing arrangements.

(b) Behavior analysts' fee practices are consistent with law and behavior analysts do not misrepresent their fees. If limitations to services can be anticipated because of limitations in financing, this is discussed with the patient, client, or other appropriate recipient of services as early as is feasible.

2.13 Accuracy in Reports to Those Who Pay for Services.

In their reports to those who pay for services or sources of research, project, or program funding, behavior analysts accurately state the nature of the research or service provided, the fees or charges, and where applicable, the identity of the provider, the findings, and other required descriptive data.

2.14 Referrals and Fees.

When a behavior analyst pays, receives payment from, or divides fees with another professional other than in an employer-employee relationship, the referral shall be disclosed to the client.

2.15 Interrupting or Terminating Services.

(a) Behavior analysts make reasonable efforts to plan for facilitating care in the event that behavior analytic services are interrupted by factors such as the behavior analyst's illness, impending death, unavailability, or relocation or by the client's relocation or financial limitations.

(b) When entering into employment or contractual relationships, behavior analysts provide for orderly and appropriate resolution of responsibility for client care in the event that the employment or contractual relationship ends, with paramount consideration given to the welfare of the client.

(c) Behavior analysts do not abandon clients. Behavior analysts terminate a professional relationship when it becomes reasonably clear that the client no longer needs the service, is not benefiting, or is being harmed by continued service.

(d) Prior to termination for whatever reason, except where precluded by the client's conduct, the behavior analyst discusses the client's views and needs, provides appropriate pre-termination services, suggests alternative service providers as appropriate, and takes other reasonable steps to facilitate transfer of responsibility to another provider if the client needs one immediately.

3.0 ASSESSING BEHAVIOR.

Behavior analysts who use behavioral assessment techniques do so for purposes that are appropriate in light of the research.

(a) Behavior analysts' assessments, recommendations, reports, and evaluative statements are based on information and techniques sufficient to provide appropriate substantiation for their findings.

(b) Behavior analysts refrain from misuse of assessment techniques, interventions, results, and interpretations and take reasonable steps to prevent others from misusing the information these techniques provide.

(c) Behavior analysts recognize limits to the certainty with which judgments or predictions can be made about individuals.

(d) Behavior analysts do not promote the use of behavioral assessment techniques by unqualified persons, i.e., those who are unsupervised by experienced professionals and have not demonstrated valid and reliable assessment skills.

3.01 Environmental Conditions that Preclude Implementation.

If environmental conditions preclude implementation of a behavior analytic program, the behavior analyst recommends that other professional assistance (i.e., assessment, consultation or therapeutic intervention by other professionals) be sought.

3.02 Environmental Conditions that Hamper Implementation.

If environmental conditions hamper implementation of the behavior analytic program, the behavior analyst seeks to eliminate the environmental constraints, or identifies in writing the obstacles to doing so.

3.03 Functional Assessment.

(a) The behavior analyst conducts a functional assessment, as defined below, to provide the necessary data to develop an effective behavior change program.

(b) Functional assessment includes a variety of systematic information-gathering activities regarding factors influencing the occurrence of a behavior (e.g., antecedents, consequences, setting events, or establishing operations) including interview, direct observation, and experimental analysis.

3.04 Accepting Clients.

The behavior analyst accepts as clients only those individuals or entities (agencies, firms, etc.) whose behavior problems or requested service are commensurate with the behavior analyst's education, training, and experience. In lieu of these conditions, the behavior analyst must function under the supervision of or in consultation with a behavior analyst whose credentials permit working with such behavior problems or services.

3.05 Consent-Client Records.

The behavior analyst obtains the written consent of the client or client-surrogate before obtaining or disclosing client records from or to other sources.

3.06 Describing Program Objectives.

(a) The behavior analyst describes, preferably in writing, the objectives of the behavior change program to the client or client-surrogate (see below) before attempting to implement the program.

(b) As used here, client-surrogate refers to someone legally empowered to make decisions for the person(s) whose behavior the program is intended to change; examples of client-surrogates include parents of minors, guardians, legally designated representatives.

3.07 Behavioral Assessment Approval.

The behavior analyst must obtain the client's or client-surrogate's approval in writing of the behavior assessment procedures before implementing them.

3.08 Describing Conditions for Program Success.

The behavior analyst describes to the client or client-surrogate the environmental conditions that are necessary for the program to be effective.

3.09 Explaining Assessment Results.

Unless the nature of the relationship is clearly explained to the person being assessed in advance and precludes provision of an explanation of results (such as in some organizational consulting, some screenings, and forensic evaluations), behavior analysts ensure that an explanation of the results is provided using language that is reasonably understandable to the person assessed or to another legally authorized person on behalf of the client. Regardless of whether the interpretation is done by the behavior analyst, by assistants, others, behavior analysts take reasonable steps to ensure that appropriate explanations of results are given.

4.0 THE BEHAVIOR ANALYST AND THE INDIVIDUAL BEHAVIOR CHANGE PROGRAM.

The behavior analyst designs programs that are based on behavior analytic principles, including assessments of effects of other intervention methods, involves the client or the client-surrogate in the planning of such programs, obtains the consent of the client, and respects the right of the client to terminate services at any time.

4.01 Approving Interventions.

The behavior analyst must obtain the client's or client-surrogate's approval in writing of the behavior intervention procedures before implementing them.

4.02 Reinforcement/Punishment.

The behavior analyst recommends reinforcement rather than punishment whenever possible. If punishment procedures are necessary, the behavior analyst always includes reinforcement procedures for alternative behavior in the program.

4.03 Avoiding Harmful Reinforcers.

The behavior analyst minimizes the use of items as potential reinforcers that may be harmful to the long-term health of the client or participant (e.g., cigarettes, or sugar or fat-laden food), or that may require undesirably marked deprivation procedures as establishing operations.

4.04 On-Going Data Collection.

The behavior analyst collects data, or asks the client, client-surrogate, or designated others to collect data needed to assess progress within the program.

4.05 Program Modifications.

The behavior analyst modifies the program on the basis of data.

4.06 Program Modifications Consent.

The behavior analyst explains the program modifications and the reasons for the modifications to the client or client-surrogate and obtains consent to implement the modifications.

4.07 Least Restrictive Procedures.

The behavior analyst reviews and appraises the restrictiveness of alternative interventions and always recommends the least restrictive procedures likely to be effective in dealing with a behavior problem.

4.08 Termination Criteria.

The behavior analyst establishes understandable and objective (i.e., measurable) criteria for the termination of the program and describes them to the client or client-surrogate.

4.09 Terminating Clients.

The behavior analyst terminates the relationship with the client when the established criteria for termination are attained, as in when a series of planned or revised intervention goals has been completed.

5.0 THE BEHAVIOR ANALYST AS TEACHER AND/OR SUPERVISOR.

Behavior analysts delegate to their employees, supervisees, and research assistants only those responsibilities that such persons can reasonably be expected to perform competently.

5.01 Designing Competent Training Programs.

Behavior analysts who are responsible for education and training programs seek to ensure that the programs are competently designed, provide the proper experiences, and meet the requirements for licensure, certification, or other goals for which claims are made by the program.

5.02 Limitations on Training.

Behavior analysts do not teach the use of techniques or procedures that require specialized training, licensure, or expertise in other disciplines to individuals who lack the prerequisite training, legal scope of practice, or expertise, except as these techniques may be used in behavioral evaluation of the effects of various treatments, interventions, therapies, or educational methods.

5.03 Providing Course Objectives.

The behavior analyst provides a clear description of the objectives of a course, preferably in writing, at the beginning of the course.

5.04 Describing Course Requirements.

The behavior analyst provides a clear description of the demands of the course (e.g., papers, exams, projects) at the beginning of the course.

5.05 Describing Evaluation Requirements.

The behavior analyst provides a clear description of the requirements for the evaluation of student performance at the beginning of the course.

5.06 Providing Feedback to Students/Supervisees.

The behavior analyst provides feedback regarding the performance of a student or supervisee as frequently as the conditions allow.

5.07 Providing Behavior Analysis Principles in Teaching.

The behavior analyst utilizes as many principles of behavior analysis in teaching a course as the material, conditions, and academic policies allow.

5.08 Requirements of Supervisees.

The behavior analyst's behavioral requirements of a supervisee must be in the behavioral repertoire of the supervisee. If the behavior required is not in the supervisee's repertoire, the behavior analyst attempts to provide the conditions for the acquisition of the required behavior, and refers the supervisee for remedial skill development services, or provides them with such services, permitting them to meet at least minimal behavioral performance requirements.

5.09 Training and Supervision.

Behavior analysts provide proper training and supervision to their employees or supervisees and take reasonable steps to see that such persons perform services responsibly, competently, and ethically. If institutional policies, procedures, or practices prevent fulfillment of this obligation, behavior analysts attempt to modify their role or to correct the situation to the extent feasible.

5.10 Feedback to Supervisees.

The behavior analyst provides feedback to the supervisee in a way that increases the probability that the supervisee will benefit from the feedback.

5.11 Reinforcing Supervisee Behavior.

The behavior analyst uses positive reinforcement as frequently as the behavior of the supervisee and the environmental conditions allow.

6.0 THE BEHAVIOR ANALYST AND THE WORKPLACE.

The behavior analyst adheres to job commitments, assesses employee interactions before intervention, works within his/her scope of training, develops interventions that benefit employees, and resolves conflicts within these Guidelines.

6.01 Job Commitments.

The behavior analyst adheres to job commitments made to the employing organization.

6.02 Assessing Employee Interactions.

The behavior analyst assesses the behavior-environment interactions of the employees before designing behavior analytic programs.

6.03 Preparing for Consultation.

The behavior analyst implements or consults on behavior management programs for which the behavior analyst has been adequately prepared.

6.04 Employees' Interventions.

The behavior analyst develops interventions that benefit the employees as well as management.

6.05 Employee Health and Well Being.

The behavior analyst develops interventions that enhance the health and well being of the employees.

6.06 Conflicts with Organizations.

If the demands of an organization with which behavior analysts are affiliated conflict with these Guidelines, behavior analysts clarify the nature of the conflict, make known their commitment to these Guidelines, and to the extent feasible, seek to resolve the conflict in a way that permits the fullest adherence to these Guidelines.

7.0 THE BEHAVIOR ANALYST AND RESEARCH.

Behavior analysts design, conduct, and report research in accordance with recognized standards of scientific competence and ethical research. Behavior analysts conduct research with human and non-human research participants according to the proposal approved by the local human research committee, and Institutional Review Board.

(a) Behavior analysts plan their research so as to minimize the possibility that results will be misleading.

(b) Behavior analysts conduct research competently and with due concern for the dignity and welfare of the participants. Researchers and assistants are permitted to perform only those tasks for which they are appropriately trained and prepared.

(c) Behavior analysts are responsible for the ethical conduct of research conducted by them or by others under their supervision or control.

(d) Behavior analysts conducting applied research conjointly with provision of clinical or human services obtain required external reviews of proposed clinical research and observe requirements for both intervention and research involvement by client-participants.

(e) In planning research, behavior analysts consider its ethical acceptability under these Guidelines. If an ethical issue is unclear, behavior analysts seek to resolve the issue through consultation with institutional review boards, animal care and use committees, peer consultations, or other proper mechanisms.

7.01 Scholarship and Research.

(a) The behavior analyst engaged in study and research is guided by the conventions of the science of behavior including the emphasis on the analysis of individual behavior and strives to model appropriate applications in professional life.

(b) Behavior analysts take reasonable steps to avoid harming their clients, research participants, students, and others with whom they work, and to minimize harm where it is foreseeable and unavoidable. Harm is defined here as negative effects or side effects of behavior analysis that outweigh positive effects in the particular instance, and that are behavioral or physical and directly observable.

(c) Because behavior analysts' scientific and professional judgments and actions affect the lives of others, they are alert to and guard against personal, financial, social, organizational, or political factors that might lead to misuse of their influence.

(d) Behavior analysts do not participate in activities in which it appears likely that their skills or data will be misused by others, unless corrective mechanisms, i.e., peer or external professional or independent review, are available.

(e) Behavior analysts do not exaggerate claims for effectiveness of particular procedures or of behavior analysis in general.

(f) If behavior analysts learn of misuse or misrepresentation of their individual work products, they take reasonable and feasible steps to correct or minimize the misuse or misrepresentation.

7.02 Using Confidential Information for Didactic or Instructive Purposes.

(a) Behavior analysts do not disclose in their writings, lectures, or other public media, confidential, personally identifiable information concerning their individual or organizational clients, students, research participants, or other recipients of their services that they obtained during the course of their work, unless the person or organization has consented in writing or unless there is other ethical or legal authorization for doing so.

(b) Ordinarily, in such scientific and professional presentations, behavior analysts disguise confidential information concerning such persons or organizations so that they are not individually identifiable to others and so that discussions do not cause harm to participants who might identify themselves.

7.03 Conforming with Laws and Regulations.

Behavior analysts plan and conduct research in a manner consistent with federal and state law and regulations, as well as professional standards governing the conduct of research, and particularly those standards governing research with human participants and animal subjects.

7.04 Informed Consent.

(a) Using language that is reasonably understandable to participants, behavior analysts inform participants of the nature of the research; they inform participants that they are free to participate or to decline to participate or to withdraw from the research; they explain the foreseeable consequences of declining or withdrawing; they inform participants of significant factors that may be expected to influence their willingness to participate (such as risks, discomfort, adverse effects, or limitations on confidentiality, except as provided in Standard 7.05 below); and they explain other aspects about which the prospective participants inquire.

(b) For persons who are legally incapable of giving informed consent, behavior analysts nevertheless (1) provide an appropriate explanation, (2) discontinue research if the person gives clear signs of unwillingness to continue participation, and (3) obtain appropriate permission from a legally authorized person, if such substitute consent is permitted by law.

7.05 Deception in Research.

(a) Behavior analysts do not conduct a study involving deception unless they have determined that the use of deceptive techniques is justified by the study's prospective scientific, educational, or applied value and that equally effective alternative procedures that do not use deception are not feasible.

(b) Behavior analysts never deceive research participants about significant aspects that would affect their willingness to participate, such as physical risks, discomfort, or unpleasant emotional experiences.

(c) Any other deception that is an integral feature of the design and conduct of an experiment must be explained to participants as early as is feasible, preferably at the conclusion of their participation, but no later than at the conclusion of the research.

7.06 Informing of Future Use.

Behavior analysts inform research participants of their anticipated sharing or further use of personally identifiable research data and of the possibility of unanticipated future uses.

7.07 Minimizing Interference.

In conducting research, behavior analysts interfere with the participants or environment from which data are collected only in a manner that is warranted by an appropriate research design and that is consistent with behavior analysts' roles as scientific investigators.

7.08 Commitments to Research Participants.

Behavior analysts take reasonable measures to honor all commitments they have made to research participants.

7.09 Ensuring Participant Anonymity.

In presenting research, the behavior analyst ensures participant anonymity unless specifically waived by the participant or surrogate.

7.10 Informing of Withdrawal.

The behavior analyst informs the participant that withdrawal from the research may occur at any time without penalty except as stipulated in advance, as in fees contingent upon completing a project.

7.11 Debriefing.

The behavior analyst informs the participant that debriefing will occur on conclusion of the participant's involvement in the research.

7.12 Answering Research Questions.

The behavior analyst answers all questions of the participant about the research that are consistent with being able to conduct the research.

7.13 Written Consent.

The behavior analyst must obtain the written consent of the participant or surrogate before beginning the research.

7.14 Extra Credit.

If the behavior analyst recruits participants from classes and the participants are provided additional credit for participating in the research, nonparticipating students must be provided alternative activities that generate comparable credit.

7.15 Acknowledging Contributions.

In presenting research, the behavior analyst acknowledges the contributions of others who contributed to the conduct of the research by including them as co-authors or footnoting their contributions.

7.16 Principal Authorship and Other Publication Credits.

Principal authorship and other publication credits accurately reflect the relative scientific or professional contributions of the individuals involved, regardless of their relative status. Mere possession of an institutional position, such as Department Chair, does not justify authorship credit. Minor contributions to the research or to the writing for publications are appropriately acknowledged, such as in footnotes or in an introductory statement. Further, these Guidelines recognize and support the ethical requirements for authorship and publication practices contained in the ethical code of the American Psychological Association.

7.17 Paying Participants.

The behavior analyst who pays participants for research involvement or uses money as a reinforcer must obtain Institutional Review Board or

Human Rights Committee approval of this practice and conform to any special requirements that may be established in the process of approval.

7.18 Withholding Payment.

The behavior analyst who withholds part of the money earned by the participant until the participant has completed their research involvement must inform the participant of this condition prior to beginning the experiment.

7.19 Grant Reviews.

The behavior analyst who serves on grant review panels avoids conducting any research described in grant proposals that the behavior analyst reviewed, except as replications fully crediting the prior researchers.

7.20 Animal Research.

Behavior analysts who conduct research involving animals treat them humanely and are in compliance with the Federal Animal Welfare Act.

8.0 THE BEHAVIOR ANALYST'S ETHICAL RESPONSIBILITY TO THE FIELD OF BEHAVIOR ANALYSIS.

The behavior analyst has a responsibility to support the values of the field, to disseminate knowledge to the public, to be familiar with these guidelines, and to discourage misrepresentation by non-certified individuals.

8.01 Affirming Principles.

The behavior analyst upholds and advances the values, ethics, principles, and mission of the field of behavior analysis; participation in both state and national or international behavior analysis organizations is strongly encouraged.

8.02 Disseminating Behavior Analysis.

The behavior analyst assists the profession in making behavior analysis methodology available to the general public.

8.03 Being Familiar with These Guidelines.

Behavior analysts have an obligation to be familiar with these Guidelines, other applicable ethics codes, and their application to behavior analysts' work. Lack of awareness or misunderstanding of a conduct standard is not itself a defense to a charge of unethical conduct.

8.04 Discouraging Misrepresentation by Non-Certified Individuals.

Behavior analysts discourage non-certified practitioners from misrepresenting that they are certified.

9.0 THE BEHAVIOR ANALYST'S RESPONSIBILITY TO COLLEAGUES.

Behavior analysts have an obligation to bring attention to and resolve ethical violations by colleagues, to make sure their data are accurate and presented truthfully, and they share data with colleagues.

9.01 Ethical Violations by Colleagues.

When behavior analysts believe that there may have been an ethical violation by another behavior analyst, they attempt to resolve the issue by bringing it to the attention of that individual if an informal resolution appears appropriate and the intervention does not violate any confidentiality rights that may be involved.

9.02 Accuracy of Data.

Behavior analysts do not fabricate data or falsify results in their publications. If behavior analysts discover significant errors in their published data, they take reasonable steps to correct such errors in a correction, retraction, erratum, or other appropriate publication means.

9.03 Authorship and Findings.

Behavior analysts do not present portions or elements of another's work or data as their own, even if the other work or data source is cited occasionally, nor do they omit findings that might alter others' interpretations of their work or behavior analysis in general.

9.04 Publishing Data.

Behavior analysts do not publish, as original data, data that have been previously published. This does not preclude republishing data when they are accompanied by proper acknowledgment.

9.05 Withholding Data.

After research results are published, behavior analysts do not withhold the data on which their conclusions are based from other competent professionals who seek to verify the substantive claims through reanalysis and who intend to use such data only for that purpose, provided that the confidentiality of the participants can be protected and unless legal rights concerning proprietary data preclude their release.

10.0 THE BEHAVIOR ANALYST'S ETHICAL RESPONSIBILITY TO SOCIETY.

The behavior analyst promotes the general welfare of society through the application of the principles of behavior.

10.01 Promotion in Society.

The behavior analyst should promote the application of behavior principles in society by presenting a behavioral alternative to other procedures or methods.

10.02 Scientific Inquiry.

The behavior analyst should promote the analysis of behavior per se as a legitimate field of scientific inquiry.

10.03 Public Statements.

(a) Behavior analysts comply with these Guidelines in public statements relating to their professional services, products, or publications or to the field of behavior analysis.

(b) Public statements include but are not limited to paid or unpaid advertising, brochures, printed matter, directory listings, personal resumes or curriculum vitae, interviews or comments for use in media, statements in legal proceedings, lectures and public oral presentations, and published materials.

10.04 Statements by Others.

(a) Behavior analysts who engage others to create or place public statements that promote their professional practice, products, or activities retain professional responsibility for such statements.

(b) Behavior analysts make reasonable efforts to prevent others whom they do not control (such as employers, publishers, sponsors, organizational clients, and representatives of the print or broadcast media) from making deceptive statements concerning behavior analysts' practices or professional or scientific activities.

(c) If behavior analysts learn of deceptive statements about their work made by others, behavior analysts make reasonable efforts to correct such statements.

(d) A paid advertisement relating to the behavior analyst's activities must be identified as such, unless it is already apparent from the context.

10.05 Avoiding False or Deceptive Statements.

Behavior analysts do not make public statements that are false, deceptive, misleading, or fraudulent, either because of what they state, convey, or suggest or because of what they omit, concerning their research, practice, or other work activities or those of persons or organizations with which they are affiliated. Behavior analysts claim as credentials for their behavioral work, only degrees that were primarily or exclusively behavior analytic in content.

10.06 Media Presentations.

When behavior analysts provide advice or comment by means of public lectures, demonstrations, radio or television programs, prerecorded tapes, printed articles, mailed material, or other media, they take reasonable precautions to ensure that (1) the statements are based on appropriate behavior analytic literature and practice, (2) the statements are otherwise consistent with these Guidelines, and (3) the recipients of the information are not encouraged to infer that a relationship has been established with them personally.

10.07 Testimonials.

Behavior analysts do not solicit testimonials from current clients or patients or other persons who because of their particular circumstances are vulnerable to undue influence.

10.08 In-Person Solicitation.

Behavior analysts do not engage, directly or through agents, in uninvited in-person solicitation of business from actual or potential users of services who because of their particular circumstances are vulnerable to undue influence, except that organizational behavior management or performance management services may be marketed to corporate entities regardless of their projected financial position.

Index for BACB® Guidelines for Responsible Conduct

developed by
Jon S. Bailey
Department of Psychology
Florida State University

Instructions

This Index is designed to allow you to find exact references to key words in Ethics Scenarios for Behavior Analysts as well as for any other ethical situation that you might encounter. Start by identifying key words or phrases in the ethics scenario. Then look up each key word and reference the related principles in one of the 10 sections of the BACB Guidelines. If you are unable to find any reference in the Guidelines to cover your ethical issue you will need to fall back on the Nine Core Ethical Principles from Koocher and Keith-Spiegel (1997).

---

[1]"Best practice" is also known as "most effective treatment procedures."
[2]See "disciplinary procedures."

D

E

---

[3]Please see "Disciplinary Standards" on the BACB.com website.

F

G

---

[4]Please see "Disciplinary procedures."

---

[5]See "Disciplinary procedures."

[6]Surrogate is used in place of "parent" in the Guidelines.

Ethics Scenarios for Behavior Analysts

Instructions

Read each scenario carefully. Each is based on an actual situation encountered by behavior analysts working in the field. We suggest that you first use a highlighter to mark key words or phrases in the scenario. Next, referring to your Index for BACB® Guidelines, write in the code number for each key issue highlighted and under "Principle," indicate in your own words what ethical principle is involved. Note that for each scenario, there may be three to four such principles. Finally, after reviewing all the ethical principles involved, indicate what steps you should take given the Guidelines.

SCENARIO 1

I am an ABA program supervisor. I have a preschooler who really needs lots of intervention. The family insists on mixing and matching approaches [floor time, gluten free and other diets, sensory integration, etc.]. This cuts down on the available ABA time to ten hours. I don't feel that this is enough time but have been unsuccessful so far in convincing the parents. Should I drop this child from our ABA program or give what I believe is a treatment that is insufficient?

Code No. _____ Principle _____

_____

_____

Code No. _____ Principle _____

_____

_____

Code No. _____ Principle _____

_____

_____

Code No. _____ Principle _____

_____

_____

What should you do? _____

_____

_____

SCENARIO 2

Is it always unethical to use testimonial information? What if a parent shares this information with a prospective client without your knowledge or permission?

Code No. _____ Principle _____

_____

_____

Code No. _____ Principle _____

_____

_____

Code No. _____ Principle _____

_____

_____

Code No. _____ Principle _____

_____

_____

What should you do? _____

_____

_____

SCENARIO 3

When confronting another behavior analyst that you believe is doing something unethical, what should you do if the other analyst either disagrees with what you are saying or denies that it is occurring?

Code No. _____ **Principle** _____

_____

_____

Code No. _____ **Principle** _____

_____

_____

Code No. _____ **Principle** _____

_____

_____

Code No. _____ **Principle** _____

_____

_____

What should you do? _____

_____

_____

SCENARIO 4

Kevin continues to bang his head when attempting to seek attention from his parents and teachers. The following approaches have been implemented: sensory integration recommended by the occupational therapist, deep pressure, joint compression, and jumping on a trampoline. Kevin continues to bang his head. Sign language was recommended by the speech therapist: Kevin is unable to discriminate between the signs, therefore he continues to bang his head. The use of a helmet was recommended by the physical therapist. Kevin continues to bang his head with the helmet and he has now begun to bite his fingers. The behavior specialist has now recommended shock therapy, after reviewing all the interventions, or medication. Is it ethical to use an aversive strategy at this point? How long should interventions continue to be in place before medication or shock therapy is considered?

Code No. _____ Principle _____

_____

_____

Code No. _____ Principle _____

_____

_____

Code No. _____ Principle _____

_____

_____

Code No. _____ Principle _____

_____

_____

What should you do? _____

_____

_____

SCENARIO 5

Are we always obligated to use the best practices that are scientifically proven effective treatments with no exceptions? What happens if we are a member of a team [a school Individual Education Plan (IEP) team, for example] and the team chooses to use and agrees on, despite your advice, an approach that is not supported by research?

Code No. _____ Principle _____

_____

_____

Code No. _____ Principle _____

_____

_____

Code No. _____ Principle _____

_____

_____

Code No. _____ Principle _____

_____

_____

What should you do? _____

_____

_____

SCENARIO 6

An ABA consultant has been working with a child with autism and his or her family. As the child approaches the age of three, a transition meeting is held between the early intervention program teacher and the school district. This meeting begins pleasantly, with sharing of information from both sides. However, a point comes when the ABA consultant and family actually become hostile and verbally attack school district personnel [Wham! Out of nowhere!], and it becomes obvious during the meeting that the consultant has painted the school district as the enemy who has little to no concern for the best interest of the child. I would say that because this is the first time the district has encountered ABA, their impression of ABA, from the very beginning, is not a positive one. Does this not damage the school's perception of ABA, along with the parents' perception of a school district [which they will likely be working with for the next twenty years], and in fact distract from what is in the best interest of the child? Is this typical procedure in dealing with school districts?

Code No. _____ Principle _____

_____

_____

Code No. _____ Principle _____

_____

_____

Code No. _____ Principle _____

_____

_____

Code No. _____ **Principle** _____

_____

_____

What should you do? _____

_____

_____

SCENARIO 7

As professionals in the field of education, we sometimes tend to forget that the children we work with have the right to privacy and their reports are deemed confidential. How can you politely tell another professional that to discuss a child's record without the family consent is not appropriate?

Code No. _____ **Principle** _____

_____

_____

Code No. _____ **Principle** _____

_____

_____

Code No. _____ **Principle** _____

_____

_____

Code No. _____ **Principle** _____

_____

_____

What should you do? _____

_____

_____

SCENARIO 8

What do you do when you have one member of the family who constantly "sabotages" the positive impact the behavior intervention and your input has on their child? In particular, one parent refuses to keep data, give you honest feedback, and offers no encouragement or support to the other parent who is willing to at least attempt what is asked. The uncooperative parent feels that there is nothing wrong with his or her child and that this intervention is a waste of time. How far, ethically, can you become involved in this family dispute to convince the combative parent to become supportive of what you and the cooperative parent are trying to accomplish on behalf of their child? Is termination of the case a viable option?

Code No. _____ Principle _____

_____

_____

Code No. _____ Principle _____

_____

_____

Code No. _____ Principle _____

_____

_____

Code No. _____ Principle _____

_____

_____

What should you do? _____

_____

_____

SCENARIO 9

Working in a home-based setting stirs up many ethical and boundary issues for therapists that do not occur in school or office settings. When working in a home, the family takes you into their "personal space." Additionally, when you work with someone's children, parents develop strong attachments to their children's therapist whom they are entrusting with their child's well-being. I have observed several of my colleagues develop "friendships" with the mothers of the children with whom they work. These relationships start out innocently enough. Usually it is a car ride to the grocery store, or perhaps the therapist and the parent may talk about shopping, and within a matter of a few sessions, the two people have planned lunch and a day at the mall. These plans at times have included or excluded the child. Home based therapy is very tricky and without the proper supervision and without properly-trained staff, there are many opportunities to develop inappropriate relationships that can both jeopardize the child's treatment and which engage the parent in an inappropriate manner. My question is actually a request for clarification of the boundary between therapist and the parent in a home-based situation. I am wondering if there are somewhat relaxed criteria for the dual relationship rules in working with children and in working in a home environment.

Code No. _____ **Principle** _____

_____

_____

Code No. _____ **Principle** _____

_____

_____

Code No. _____ **Principle** _____

_____

_____

Code No. _____ **Principle** _____

_____

_____

What should you do? _____

_____

_____

SCENARIO 10

Many of the requests for my services as a behavior consultant come
when agencies or schools are struggling with families and are at odds
with what to do to help a child with his or her behavior difficulties. The
agency or school provides the funding to pay for my services and is the
one who initiates my involvement with the student. At times, my review
of the case and the analysis of the data I have gathered, leads me to believe that previous interventions were not well thought out and were
primarily of a reactive nature. Indeed, they may have actually caused the
situation to become worse. Several times, families have asked me
point-blank as to the cause of the student's behavior and my opinion of
these previous interventions. How do I respond ethically, knowing that
if I share my beliefs, I risk alienating the agency or school and possibly
giving the families more reasons not to trust the people involved with
their child?

Code No. _____ Principle _____

_____

_____

Code No. _____ Principle _____

_____

_____

Code No. _____ Principle _____

_____

_____

Code No. _____ Principle _____

_____

_____

What should you do? _____

_____

_____

SCENARIO 11

The client is a nineteen-year-old girl in high school (diagnosed with mild mental retardation). She has a history of sexual abuse and was a crack baby at birth. Last month there was an incident in which it was discovered that she was not riding the school bus and was instead walking to school. The problem is that she would meet with a man and have sexual intercourse in his front yard. At that point, they had an adult female talk to her about safe sex. My supervisor suggests she be provided condoms and paid to go to a motel instead. The Home Group Manager said she would allow her to have sex in her bedroom, however, there are foster kids present and that may bring up other issues. I don't agree with directing her to a motel as a replacement behavior. I don't think she should be encouraged to have sex with strangers. She has in the past invited male strangers into the home. I am having a difficult time coming up with a replacement behavior to suit her. She has excellent communication skills and gets great grades in school.

Code No. _____ **Principle** _____

_____

_____

Code No. _____ **Principle** _____

_____

_____

Code No. _____ **Principle** _____

_____

_____

Code No. _____ **Principle** _____

_____

_____

What should you do? _____

_____

_____

Suggested Further Reading

Bersoff, D. N. (2003). *Ethical Conflicts in Psychology*. American Psychological Association, Washington, DC.

This third edition of Bersoff's text includes material on ethics codes, applying ethics, confidentiality, multiple relationships, assessment, computerized testing, therapy, and research; supervision, guidelines for animal research, ethics in forensic settings, ethical practice within the boundaries of managed care; the American Psychological Association (APA) 2002 Ethics Code; and the revisions to the Rules and Procedures for adjudicating complaints of unethical conduct against APA members adopted by the APA's Ethics Committee in August 2002.

Canter, M. B., Bennett, B. E., Jones, S. E., & Nagy, T. F. (1999). *Ethics for Psychologists: A Commentary on the APA Ethics Code*. American Psychological Association, Washington, DC.

The three main sections of this volume are Foundations, Interpreting the Ethics Code, and Conclusions. The bulk of the book is the section on "Interpreting the Ethics Code," in which each ethical standard is analyzed and commentary is provided.

Danforth, S., & Boyle, J. R. (2000). *Cases in Behavior Management.* Prentice Hall, Upper Saddle River, NJ.

This book begins by presenting social systems theory; models of treatment including the behavioral, psychodynamic, environmental, and constructivist models and information on analyzing cases. The second half of the book features 38 cases that illustrate behavior management issues faced by teachers, parents, and caregivers. A number of the vignettes are related to school settings (preschool through high school). Cases are very detailed with most being three to four pages in length.

Fisher, C. B. (2003). *Decoding the Ethics Code: A Practical Guide for Psychologists.* Sage, Thousand Oaks, CA.

The 2002 American Psychological Association's Ethical Principles of Psychologists and Code of Conduct is presented in this volume. After an introduction describing how the Code came to be developed, the foundation and application of each ethical standard is discussed along with enforcement of the code. Other topics presented include professional liability issues, ethical decision making, and the relation between ethics and law.

Hayes, L. J., Hayes, G. J., Moore, S. C., & Ghezzi, P. M. (1994). *Ethical Issues in Developmental Disabilities.* Context Press, Reno, NV.

This volume is a collection of theoretical articles by a variety of authors. Some of the topics include choice and value, moral development, morality, ethical issues concerning people with DD, competence, right to treatment, ethics and adult services, and the pharmacological treatment of behavior problems.

Jacob, S., & Hartshorne, T. S. (2003). *Ethics and the Law for School Psychologists.* Wiley, New York.

This text provides information on professional standards and legal requirements relevant to the delivery of school psychological services. Topics covered include students' and parents' rights to privacy and informed consent, confidentiality, assessment, ethical issues related to Individuals with Disabilities Education Act (IDEA) and Americans with Disabilities Act, educating children with special needs, consultation with teachers, school discipline, school violence prevention, and ethical issues in supervision. *Ethics and the Law for School Psychologists* addresses the changes in the 2002 revision of the American Psychological Association's Ethical Principles and Code of Conduct.

Koocher, G. P., & Keith-Spiegel, P. C. (1990). *Children, Ethics, and the Law: Professional Issues and Cases.* University of Nebraska Press, Lincoln.

Children, Ethics, and the Law outlines ethical and legal issues encountered by mental health workers in their work with children, adolescents, and their families. This volume addresses issues pertinent to psychotherapy with children, assessment, confidentiality and record keeping, consent to treatment and research, and legal issues. Case vignettes are provided to illustrate the ethical and legal dilemmas under discussion.

Nagy, T. F. (2000). *An Illustrative Casebook for Psychologists.* American Psychological Association, Washington, DC.

An Illustrative Casebook for Psychologists was written to accompany the 102 standards of the American Psychological Association's Ethics Committee's Ethical Principles of Psychologists and Code of Conduct. Fictional case vignettes are used throughout the text to illustrate the key areas of the APA Code, which include General Standards; Evaluation, Assessment, or Intervention; Advertising and Other Public Statements; Therapy; Privacy and Confidentiality; Teaching, Training Supervision, Research, and Publishing; Forensic Activities; and Resolving Ethical Issues.

Pope, K. S., & Vasquez, M. J. T. (1998). *Ethics in Psychotherapy and Counseling.* Jossey-Bass, San Francisco.

This text addresses areas in which ethical dilemmas occur in the work of mental health practitioners. Issues covered include informed consent, sexual and nonsexual relationships with clients, cultural and individual differences, supervisory relationships, and confidentiality. There are appendixes of codes of conduct and ethical principles for psychologists, and guidelines for ethical counseling in managed-care settings.

Stolz, S. B., et al. (1978). *Ethical Issues in Behavior Modification.* Jossey-Bass, San Francisco.

In 1974, the American Psychological Association formed a commission to examine issues related to social, legal, and ethical controversies in psychology. The commission also provided recommendations regarding the use and misuse of behavior modification. This historic volume addresses the ethics of behavior modification in settings that include outpatient settings, institutions, schools, prisons, and society. The volume also addresses the ethics of interventions.

Welfel, E. R., & Ingersoll, R. E. (2001). *The Mental Health Desk Reference.* Wiley, New York.

Part IX of *The Mental Health Desk Reference* is "Ethical and Legal Issues." This section of the text addresses procedures for filing ethics complaints, clients' rights to privacy, informed consent, responsible documentation, reporting child abuse, recognizing elder abuse, supervision, and responsible interactions with managed-care organizations.

References

American Psychological Association. (2001). *PsychSCAN: Behavior analysis & therapy*. Washington, DC: American Psychological Association.

Animal Welfare Act. (1990). 7 U.S.C. § 2131 et. seq.

Ayllon, T., & Michael, J. (1959). The psychiatric nurse as a behavioral engineer. *Journal of the Experimental Analysis of Behavior, 2,* 323–334.

BACB Professional Disciplinary Standards. (2004). *Behavior Analyst Certification Board.* Retrieved January 2, 2005 from www.bacb.com/cues/frame_about.html

Bailey, J. S., & Burch, M. R. (2002). *Research methods in applied behavior analysis.* Thousand Oaks, CA, Sage.

BBC Radio. (1999, January 26). *Ten least respected professions* [Radio]. Available from www.bbc.co.uk/pressoffice/pressreleases/stories/2002/05_May/29/respected_professions.html

Beutler, L. E. (2000). Empirically based decision making in clinical practice. *Prevention & treatment,* Volume 3, Article 27. Copyright 2000 by the American Psychological Association. www.journals.apa.org/prevention/volume3/pre0030027a.html

Binder, R. L. (1992). Sexual harassment: Issues for forensic psychiatrists. *Bulletin of the Academy of Psychiatry Law, 20,* 409–418.

Carnegie, D. (1981). *How to win friends and influence people.* New York: Pocket Books/Simon & Schuster, Inc.

Daniels, A. C. (2000). *Bringing out the best in people: How to apply the astonishing power of positive reinforcement.* New York: McGraw–Hill.

Daniels, A. C., & Daniels, J. E. (2004). *Performance management: Changing behavior that drives organizational effectiveness.* Atlanta, GA: Aubrey Daniels International, Inc.

Frederiksen, L. W. (Ed.). (1982). *Handbook of organizational behavior management.* New York: Wiley.

Harvard Classics Volume 38. (1910). P. F. Collier and Son.

Hill, A. (1998). *Speaking truth to power.* New York: Anchor.

Holland, J. G., & Skinner, B. F. (1961). *The analysis of behavior: A program for self-instruction.* New York: McGraw-Hill.

Iwata, B. A., Dorsey, M. F., Slifer, K. J., Bauman, K. E., & Richman, G. S. (1982). Toward a functional analysis of self-injury. *Analysis and Intervention in Developmental Disabilities, 2,* 3–20.

Koocher, G. P., & Keith-Spiegel, P. (1998). *Ethics in psychology: Professional standards and cases* (2nd ed.). New York: Oxford University Press.

Krasner, L., & Ullmann, L. P. (Eds.). (1965). *Research in behavior modification.* New York: Holt, Rinehart and Winston, Inc.

McAllister, J. W. (1972). *Report of resident abuse investigating committee.* Tallahassee: Division of Retardation, Department of Health and Rehabilitative Services.

Neuringer, C., & Michael, J. L. (Eds.). (1970). *Behavior modification in clinical psychology.* New York: Apple-Century-Crofts.

O'Brien, R. M., Dickinson, A. M., & Rosow, M. P. (Eds.). (1982). *Industrial behavior modification: A management handbook.* New York: Pergamon.

OCR Summary of the HIPAA Privacy Rule. (2003). *United States Department of Health & Human Services.* Retrieved January 2, 2005, from www.hhs.gov/ocr/hipaa/privacy.html

Ontario Consultants on Religious Tolerance. (2004). Kingston, ON, Canada.

Singer, M. T., & Lalich, J. (1996). *Crazy therapies: What are they? Do they work?* San Francisco: Jossey-Bass.

Skinner, B. F. (1953). *Science and human behavior.* New York: Macmillan.

Skinner, B. F. (1957). *Verbal behavior.* New York: Appleton-Century-Crofts.

Ullmann, L. P., & Krasner, L. (Eds.). (1965). *Case studies in behavior modification.* New York: Holt, Rinehart and Winston, Inc.

United States Equal Employment Opportunity Commission. (2004). *Sexual harassment charges: EEOC & FEPA s combined: FY 1992–FY 2003.*

Van Houten, R., Axelrod, S., Bailey, J. S., Favell, J. E., Foxx, R. M., Iwata, B. A., et al. (1988). The right to effective behavioral treatment. *Journal of Applied Behavior Analysis, 21,* 381–384.

Wolf, M., Risley, R., & Mees, H. (1964). Application of operant conditioning procedures to the behaviour problems of an autistic child. *Behaviour Research and Therapy, 1,* 305–312.

Wyatt v. Stickney. 325 F. Supp 781 (M.D. Ala. 1971).

Author Index

Subject Index